YOU'LL SEE JESUS ON MY FACE

You'll See Jesus on My Face

ISBN: 978-1-60920-014-5

Cover design by Isaac Publishing, Inc.

Library of Congress Control Number: 2011920482

Printed in the United States of America

Publication sponsored by the
Kokomo Rescue Mission

IPI
Isaac Publishing, Inc.
P.O. 342
Three Rivers, MI 49093
www.isaacpublishing.com

Please direct your inquiries to admin@isaacpublishing.com

You'll See Jesus on My Face

Cynthia Burch
As told to Riley B. Case

Ephesians 6:10-20

"Finally, be strong in the Lord and in his mighty power. Put on the full armor of God so that you can take your stand against the devil's schemes. For our struggle is not against flesh and blood, but against the rulers, against the authorities, against the powers of this dark world and against the spiritual forces of evil in the heavenly realms. Therefore put on the full armor of God, so that when the day of evil comes, you may be able to stand your ground, and after you have done everything, to stand. Stand firm then, with the belt of truth buckled around your waist, with the breastplate of righteousness in place, and with your feet fitted with the readiness that comes from the gospel of peace. In addition to all this, take up the shield of faith, with which you can extinguish all the flaming arrows of the evil one. Take the helmet of salvation and the sword of the Spirit, which is the word of God. And pray in the Spirit on all occasions with all kinds of prayers and requests. With this in mind, be alert and always keep on praying for all the saints. Pray also for me, that whenever I open my mouth, words may be given me so that I will fearlessly make known the mystery of the gospel, for which I am an ambassador in chains. Pray that I may declare it fearlessly, as I should."

Contents

Foreword

Pastors receive many phone calls. One of the many features available on even the most basic cell phone is caller identification. Usually, if I don't recognize the caller number, I simply don't answer… but there are exceptions. In the summer of 2010 I deviated from my usual protocol and accepted the call from a number that I did not recognize. It was Cynthia Burch. She wanted to discuss her upcoming presentation at Parr United Methodist Church, a small but caring congregation located at the north end of Kokomo. We agreed to meet at a local restaurant to deliberate. Having never met Cynthia in person I asked how I might recognize her. She simply replied, **"Oh, I will be the girl with the long brown hair and you'll see Jesus on my face."**

Needless to say I could hardly wait to meet this person who actually wore the countenance of our Savior for everyone to witness. This book is Cynthia's recollection of her encounters with the dark forces of today's drug culture. It is an authentic recount of her disjointed, confusing life, told as she remembers it. Her story is not fiction; it is real. Her story is about addiction, rejection, loneliness, desperation and redemption. It is a compelling read which promises hope for the helpless, and how hope changes everything. I trust that as you read, you will be just as excited as I was to meet **"The girl with Jesus on her face."**

—B. J. Siefert Pastor, Parr United
Methodist Church, Kokomo, IN

It was right after Independence Day in 2009. I had been the Director of Women's Ministries at Open Arms, a ministry of the Kokomo Rescue Mission, for almost 5 years, when I saw Cynthia standing in the hallway. I knew she was supposed to come to Open Arms, placed by the Drug Court Program. We had read the reports from Richmond State Hospital that she had some successes there. The question that kept popping in my head was, '"Has she REALLY changed?" After all, she had been at Open

Arms on five different occasions, and she was not exactly the model resident. The last time she was told she could not return.

I saw a beautiful woman with a beautiful complexion, and a smile on her face, and I had to ask Ms. Krista, "Who is that woman?" Ms. Krista replied, "Cynthia Burch." My mouth fell to the ground; that couldn't be Cythnia Burch, could it? I walked up to her and she turned around; her long brown hair swung around with her body and she said, "Hello, Ms. Kem." I was so excited; I hugged her and said, "I couldn't believe it is you. You are so beautiful."

She had a glow about her that I can't explain. As I got to know Cynthia better, I told her that she was a pretty gal, but "her insides were prettier than her outsides!" Her ability in dealing with people has to be a gift from God. She has such a compassionate heart and she puts herself in each of the guest's shoes, probably because she has been in their shoes! She listens to each guest and then she prays for them. She tells them how she made it through all of her struggles and that Jesus is the only answer to their problems.

Cynthia was not the only guest living at Open Arms. While she was at Open Arms, at various times we also housed and served 150 other women and their children. Each person is an individual with individual needs. Maybe the woman that is sitting across from my desk needs her GED, or higher education; maybe that woman needs more parenting skills, or help getting off drugs or alcohol. Each woman that God has placed at Open Arms has her own unique story, just like Cynthia.

This story is about Cynthia, but more importantly it's about what God has done in Cynthia's life. It is about how He has protected her and how He helped her through each situation. It is how He placed the right people around her, just when she needed each one.

While Cynthia stayed at Open Arms, she would walk through the halls singing, *I am free to love; I am free to dance; I am free to live for You. I am free.* Cynthia did not just mean she was free from the Howard County Jail. She was free from the bondage of sin, sin that led to addiction, destruction, and loss. Cynthia learned that the only way out of that bondage is through the blood of Jesus Christ and a relationship with Him.

—Kem Howell, Director of Open ArmsKokomo Rescue Mission

Addiction is a terrible thing. That phrase sounds so trite, but most of us will never know how horribly true it is. I've been actively engaged in the criminal justice system for over thirty years. I've prosecuted and defended women with addictions. I've watched as they chose their addiction over their relationship with spouses. I've watched as they chose their addiction over all of their worldly possessions. I've watched as they chose their addiction over food for themselves and their children. I've watched as they sold their bodies to pursue their addiction. I've watched as they committed crimes to pursue their addiction.

Cynthia used to be one of those women. Her first brush with the law came after she forged her sister's name in order to obtain medical treatment. Later she was charged with neglect of a dependent; sometime later she was arrested for possession of a controlled substance. Cynthia was required to serve six months on In-home detention, followed by eighteen months of supervised probation. She was ordered to complete the Court's Drug and Alcohol Program. She violated the terms of In-home, of probation, and was non-compliant with treatment. She continued committing crimes, including neglect of a dependent, and possession of a methamphetamine. She lost her children. She was facing well over twenty years in prison.

Through a series of events, Cynthia turned her life around. She has been participating in the Drug Court Program, and is now choosing life over addiction. Hopefully, her story will help others make the same choice.

—William C. Menges, Jr.
Judge, Howard Superior Court I
Kokomo, IN

"God spoke to me today. There was this lady-bug...."

If you were ever greeted with a comment like that it is quite likely the speaker was Cynthia Burch. Cynthia sees God in everything: in the piece of a leaf, in a conversation, in a Bible verse, in a song, or in a tomato sandwich.

If you are so blessed you will have encouragement for the day.

It was not always that way, of course. This book tells why. I believe the story is so compelling it will be hard to put down once it is begun.

The title of the book, *You'll See Jesus On My Face,* might appear to be presumptuous if used for almost any other person. Not so with Cynthia. She, and others who know her, believe the title reflects accurately what you sense when you meet Cynthia for the first time, or spend much time around her.

I count it a privilege to be part of the telling of this story. As I listened to her recount this story in conversation and on tape recorder, sometimes laughing and sometimes crying, I found myself laughing and crying with her. Then I laughed and cried again as I transcribed the words to writing.

I also count it a privilege to be a part of the Kokomo Rescue Mission. The reason this ministry accepts almost no tax money is so that we can be free to live and proclaim without restriction the uniqueness of Jesus Christ. We can refer to numbers of testimonies like Cynthia's, though most are not as dramatic. At the same time "the mission" has an excellent working relationship with the other social service organizations in Kokomo, with other social services, with the Drug Court Program, and with city agencies. We also are thankful for the support of the churches. Churches of every theological stripe offer their prayers, their volunteer helpers, and their financial support to make the ministry possible.

You'll See Jesus on My Face is a descriptive title for the story of Cynthia Burch. But in another sense it is also a descriptive title for the story of the Kokomo Rescue Mission. For more than fifty-five years the mission has sought to be the face of Jesus in Kokomo and the six-county surrounding area. Persons in the Kokomo area remember the 16-feet tall likeness of Jesus painted on plywood that for many years marked the mission at its location along Washington Street in Kokomo. It was a city landmark. This was replaced, when the new mission building was dedicated in 1998, by a fourteen feet-tall limestone relief sculpture of Jesus as the Good Shepherd embedded at the corner of the building. It looks

out over a city that we claim for God.
You'll See Jesus on Our Face.

Riley Case, President
Board of Directors
Kokomo Rescue Mission

Introduction and Acknowledgements

When I was a little girl I wished for a bullhorn so I could speak and be heard. I wanted to tell someone things going on in my mind.

Well, I didn't have a bullhorn. But even if I had, who would have listened? I didn't have any close friends that I felt free to talk to or confide in. Part of it was my fault since I didn't trust anyone. So I never spoke of the things going on inside me—not to my parents, or to my sisters, or to the teachers, or to the kids at school. I had the feeling that if I told others anything they would laugh at me, or they wouldn't believe me. I composed some poems but I didn't share them with anyone. I sometimes used to wonder if I died whether anyone would really know who I was. If I did die, would anyone attend the funeral?

I lived my life in the world of drugs and in that world we didn't express our feelings; drugs were our escape, to keep us from having to deal with feelings. I lived that life for a long time.

Then I had this conversion. Jesus came into my life. Now I really did have something to talk about. Jesus. Happiness. Now I couldn't keep quiet. I wanted others to know about it. I longed for that bullhorn. I was in jail at the time so I talked to the only people who were available to me—my jail mates. I talked; I sang; I witnessed. Some of them must have thought I *was* a bullhorn, disturbing the peace. I remember some of them saying, "Cynthia, it is too early in the morning." I began to write some things—poems, letters.

When I got out of jail I was more careful. I didn't have a captive audience. Drug court didn't want too much of Jesus in its sessions. Not everyone was interested in my story.

Then one day someone was. When I graduated from Open Arms, Riley Case, president of the Kokomo Rescue Mission Board, was the one who gave me my diploma. I gave a brief testimony. He asked me if I would share it at the church he attended, Greentown United Methodist Church. He and his wife Ruth asked me to their home. I met some of their family.

Then he asked if I would be interested in telling my story—like in a book. He would help write it.

Was I interested? Wow! Maybe I would get my bullhorn after all. Riley would be my bullhorn.

Then I had second thoughts. How much did I really want to tell? How much did I want to tell him? What would he think? Riley was a retired preacher. I didn't know if my story was fit for a preacher.

The Cases had me to their home. I worked with Riley in his garden. I pruned trees and transplanted amaranthus seedlings and pulled weeds and drove a tractor. Riley talked about birds and plants and first fruits and too much rain. He wanted me to learn bird songs.

That helped me to feel comfortable. Soon I was blurting it all out, even the painful parts. Stuff started coming out from deep inside me, and coming, and coming. If there is ugly stuff it is only so that the story can lead to grace—amazing, wonderful grace.

My story is not about me. It is about an awesome God. I want Him to have all the glory. This book is like my bullhorn, my chance to tell about the Good Shepherd who seeks and brings home the one lost sheep.

The story is also about answered prayer, especially the prayer I prayed in jail that God would put the right people in my life. These are the people you will read about in this book. They are jail mates, policemen, judges, counselors, attorneys. They are people at the Kokomo Rescue Mission and at Open Arms. I thank every one of them for what they have meant in my life and for making this book possible.

—Cynthia

CHAPTER 1

I Am Not Cindy Burch

Give thanks to the Lord, for he is good;
His love endures forever.
Let the redeemed of the Lord say this—
Those he redeemed from the hand of the foe…
—Psalm 107:1, 2

I am not Cindy Burch. Cindy Burch is that woman whose name was in *The Kokomo Perspective* five times between 1999 and 2008. Each week *The Perspective* prints the names of those who have been arrested. Cindy Burch was arrested for possession of liquid hydrocodone, for possession of meth, for theft, for stolen identity, for violation of probation, for child neglect, and for possession of a syringe. Several times *The Perspective* ran her picture. She was not pretty in those pictures. Her hair was unkempt; her teeth were rotting; she looked defiant. …I am not Cindy Burch.

Teachers at school knew Cindy Burch. She came to school dirty, when she even came. She was sullen. She failed many of her courses. She would swear and talk dirty. She ran the streets. She dealt drugs. The kids avoided her. The bullies bullied her. She got into fights. …I am not Cindy Burch.

Cindy Birch was the girl who would trade sex for a place to stay, or for food, or for drugs. Among certain men her name was known. …I am not Cindy Burch.

Cindy Burch named her daughter Crystal—Crystal Faith—in honor of meth crystals. Meth crystals were Cindy's god. It was what she lived for. ...I am not Cindy Burch.

Judge Menges knew Cindy Burch. After all, he saw her maybe fifteen times. Five times she was sent to jail. The Cindy Burch Judge Menges dealt with was angry, unrepentant, unruly, and unattractive. ...I am not Cindy Burch.

Cindy Burch lived in filth. The houses she stayed in were so dirty you could get dirty just walking across the room. They smelled. Cindy Burch lived like a wild animal. Drugs took the place of cleanliness and health and warmth. ...I am not Cindy Burch.

Cindy Burch was a stripper. She worked almost all the clubs in Kokomo. She had no modesty. She had no regard for her body. A lot of men knew Cindy Burch. ...I am not Cindy Burch.

Cindy Burch needed $2,000 a day for her drug habit. She got it any way she could. She was good at cooking meth. She lived for drugs. Drugs came before her health, her self-respect, her friendships, and even her children. ...I am not Cindy Burch.

Cindy Burch was a slave, a slave to powers of darkness, a slave to evil forces, and to Satan. There was no light in the life of Cindy Burch; it was all darkness. ...I am not Cindy Burch.

Cindy Burch died. She died three times. She overdosed in front of her own kids. She lay on the laundry room floor. Her 9-year old daughter tried to wake her up: "Mommy, Mommy!" There was no movement. The boyfriend called 911. The paramedics came. They gave Cindy Burch a shot of adrenalin. She revived, but her heart stopped two more times that evening. Once she was pronounced dead. ...I am not Cindy Burch.

Whatever happened to Cindy Burch? The Cindy Burch, that is, that many people remembered before 2008?

Cindy Burch died. Cindy Burch died, and is dead. This was a different death from the death in the laundry room. This time Cindy Burch died a spiritual death; Cindy Burch died to sin. It happened in a jail cell, a cold, hard jail cell.

Some sat in darkness and the deepest gloom,
Prisoners suffering in iron chains,
for they had rebelled against the words of God
and despised the counsel of the Most High....

Then they cried to the Lord in their trouble...

—Psalm 107:11

Cindy Burch cried to Jesus and Jesus came. Jesus entered that jail cell and gathered all of the sin and the ugliness and the bitterness and the shame and the loneliness and the hatred that was Cindy Burch—and took it upon himself. He took the judgment and the death that were due her and nailed it to his cross, the cross he bore up Calvary's hill. On that cross He died. It was an ugly death. It was a crucifixion. The sky was blackened; the earth shook. But the price was paid. The price for sin. Jesus died and was buried. He did this for Cindy Burch. And when he died and was buried Cindy Birch also died and was buried.

Whatever happened to Cindy Burch? Cindy Burch rose from the dead with Jesus who is the Christ. That is, the new Cindy Burch rose with Jesus. Cindy Burch rose a new creature, even as it is written: "If anyone is in Christ, she is a new creation." What about her sin? It is gone, buried, and forgotten. What about the spiritual bonds that held her captive? Those bonds were broken. What of Satan, who owned her? He was defeated.

He brought them out of darkness and deepest gloom,
And he saved them from their distress.
And broke away their chains.

—Psalm 107: 19, 20

People may remember the old Cindy Burch; they may remember who she was and what she did. They may remember curses and anger and defiance. But God does not see the old Cindy Burch. God does not even remember Cindy Burch and the sin. God does not remember the sin because it is covered by the blood of Jesus. That is the promise of the Bible: "I will remember their sin no more" (Jeremiah 31:33).

Whatever happened to Cindy Burch? Cindy Burch is now Cynthia Burch. When Cindy Burch became a new creature she was given a new name. Actually it was the name she was always supposed to have—Cynthia Burch. Jesus lifted her up and called her Cynthia.

Cynthia Burch is now a child of God, loved, forgiven, and valued. The old Cindy Burch went around with head bowed. The new Cynthia Burch can hold up her head because she is valued. And on her face you can see Jesus.

Who is this Cynthia Burch? Let me introduce her. I am Cynthia Burch, and this is my story.

Let them give thanks to the Lord for his unfailing love
And his wonderful works for men,
For he breaks down gates of bronze
And cuts through bars of iron. —Psalm 107:15, 16

CHAPTER 2

Daddy, Daddy

"Get down here."

We dreaded those words, my sisters and I. We trembled, and came. Not to come was not an option.

"Line up."

I don't know why daddy was mad this time. We didn't move fast enough; or we disobeyed. Sometimes there was no reason.

"I thought I told you….."

Fill in the blank. It could be for any reason.

His belt was out. The flailing began. One by one. On this occasion I happened to be first. It was not a cuff with an open hand. It was not like a spanking. It was not an effort to sting to emphasize a moment of discipline. It was a beating. Perhaps more like a flogging.

The pain was unbearable. Across the bottom. Another strike, this one on the legs. Another strike, up the back. Daddy was not always a good aim. If it had been a whip and not a belt it would have cut through what clothes we had on; it would have torn flesh. As it was it raised bruises and welts and sometimes drew blood.

I was determined not to cry, but it didn't work. I was sobbing. The blows kept coming, one after another. Would I die? When the beatings came that thought would pass through my mind. If I had known God I would have cried for mercy, for relief, for help. Perhaps my cries were like prayers, addressed to God. Surely He heard. "Please make it stop."

Finally he was done with me. It was my sister's turn. All my sisters screamed. Would the neighbors check to see what was the matter?

No, they never did. Would my mom say anything at all, urge any kind of restraint, or say something like, "That is enough"?

She never did. She let it happen. She was a submissive wife. There was no reason why he would not turn on her as well as the children.

I stood over on the side. I could not sit. I believe I suffered as much for my sisters as for myself.

"No...no...please no..."

Pleading did not help. If anything it would lengthen the number of hits. The horrible sound stays with me today. No wonder it has taken so long to heal.

Would it ever stop?

It stopped finally for Carolyn. Maybe he wasn't so hard on Carolyn. Carolyn was slow in school. Maybe there was some pity on daddy's part. There was no pity for the rest of us. It was Loretta's turn. The same screaming, the sobbing, the blows, one after another. He swung harder, as if he couldn't make it hurt enough. We were all sobbing. Then it happened to Debbie. We were not only beaten ourselves. We had to watch each other take the beatings.

That was not the only time. It happened regularly. I don't even know how often. Maybe each one was so terrible it seems there were more times than there were.

I remember one time in the bathroom. My dad made us pull down our pants. He hit us on the bare skin. We would go to my mom for help. She did nothing. She said, "There is nothing I can do."

When it was over we found our own quiet places to sob in. We would not talk about it. We were too ashamed perhaps. Maybe we were too crushed. For the beatings not only bruised the body, they bruised our spirits, and our souls. How could any of us ever believe she was a child of God if she was made to feel worthless and deserving of beating after beating after beating?

The beating was only part of it. He called us names. His favorite name for us was "bees." He told us we would be *whores* and *sluts* like our mother. There was always cursing. We were *bitches* and *sons of bitches*. He put us down before other people. We were being ground down to dust.

He told us not to tell. If we told it would be worse for us.

We lied at school. I would sometimes miss school because of the bruises. At times when I went I could hardly sit down. The teachers would ask what had happened. I would say I fell down, or I had a fight with my sister.

Daddy had a gun. He was proud of it. It was loaded. He showed us how to shoot it.

When it came out later that he was molesting us girls he would threaten us with the gun. One time he was waving the gun. He had been confronted with the molesting. He said, "If this ever comes out I would have to get rid of everybody."

I was so confused. I loved my dad but I hated him.

One night I slipped out of bed. I got the gun. I went to his room and stood in the doorway. He was in bed asleep. It would be so easy to aim the gun and pull the trigger. I would go to jail but somehow that did not matter. I fingered the trigger.

I could not do it. My mom was in bed. I could not do it for her sake.

I took the gun back.

My heart ached.

I was told in Richmond when I was in counseling to go back to those moments. Go back as the adult Cynthia and hug the little girl, the child Cindy, and comfort her. I do that now. But I know that Jesus is also hugging that child Cindy.

When I was eleven I wrote my first poem. I didn't write it on paper. It was in my mind. I memorized it. I would say it over and over. I didn't feel so terrible when I could express my feelings with words. I knew it was a good poem. I couldn't be all bad if I could compose a poem. It sustained me.

Daddy, Daddy, why did you hurt me so?
I will cry at night; I will cry at day.
Daddy, won't you tell me, can't you say?
Why did you hurt me in this way.
I don't understand, I feel so confused,
My mind is rushing, I feel so abused.
Daddy, please answer this question,
Why did you do it? Why did it have to be me?

—Cindy Burch, age 11

Cynthia Burch

CHAPTER 3

Born an Alcoholic

No one ever told me I was born an alcoholic, but I am convinced I was. My mother was an alcoholic, as well as a drug addict, and she never changed what she was doing just because she was pregnant with me. There must have been a lot of alcohol going through my system when I was in the womb. What I remember is, the first time I tasted beer as a child, I liked it. I was only three years old, maybe even younger. My sisters tasted beer and spit it out. I tasted it and wanted more. It gave me a warm feeling.

My parents had a lot of friends over to our house. Maybe they were more like partying acquaintances than friends. When they found out I liked beer they would offer it to me. I would drink it. They thought that was cute. They laughed.

My mother had a habit of putting peanuts in her drink. Don't ask me why. But if she left the room I drank the wine, or beer, or whatever it was, to get the peanuts. My parents' friends found out so they started leaving peanuts in drinks on purpose. They wanted to see me drink the wine to get to the peanuts. They didn't know they were encouraging my alcoholism.

There wasn't much discipline in our home, that is, discipline that would help me to know right from wrong, or what was good for me and not good for me. There was screaming and hitting, but that wasn't discipline. My mom and my dad would be angry for some reason or other and that's when there would be screaming and hitting. Sometimes we didn't know why they were angry. They just were.

My parents didn't look after us much. They often left us alone, even when we were pre-schoolers. One day we were home alone, my sisters and I. I think I was four. There was a six-pack of beer in the refrigerator. Usually my parents didn't want us in the refrigerator or in the cupboard. That was off limits. That was reason for a beating. But on this day they weren't home and we found the six-pack. I was able to open a bottle. I began drinking it and soon it was gone. Then I opened the second bottle and drank it, then the third bottle, and the fourth, and the fifth, and finally the sixth. Why I didn't pass out from being drunk I don't know. All of this was in the period of about an hour. At that point I realized I was soon going to be in deep trouble. My older sister Carolyn had an idea. We would fill the empty bottles with water and put them back in the refrigerator. Not long after that, when my mom came home, there was an angry cry from the kitchen. My mom had discovered the water in the beer bottles. Since Carolyn was the oldest daughter she was the one who was confronted: "What happened to the beer in the bottles?" Carolyn made up a story and took the blame. "I didn't want you to drink so I dumped out all the beer."

My father used alcohol to control us, especially to put us sleep at night. Otherwise we would stay awake all night, or until we dropped. He would call me upstairs and remind me that I was a sick girl and needed medicine. The medicine was NyQuil, a cough medicine with alcohol in it. I liked it. It made me feel warm inside and made me ready for bed.

Our family was moving around a lot in those years. I was born in Kokomo, December 1, 1978, the second of four girls. Carolyn was a year older than me. Loretta was a year younger than me and Debbie was a year younger than Loretta. Just before Loretta was born we moved to Tennessee. After a while we were back in Kokomo. Then we moved to Utah where we had relatives. My dad's mother, so I am told, had been a Mormon. My dad's people were there. What I remember about them is that there was always fighting and arguing between my dad and them. One uncle, I remember, had HIV. My dad would make fun of him and degrade him about being gay. He later died of AIDS.

My uncle Bob McClure had a boy my age, Bobby, who used to bully us. He would order my sisters and me to do something and if we didn't do it he would hit us. He would hit us hard and we were afraid of him. My sisters took it and crept away but I would fight back. My dad liked that. He called me his tomboy. My sisters and I would sometimes play and have a good time together but often we fought. And we fought until we really hurt each other. My dad never intervened.

I think about those things now, years later. Are we born good or are we born with an inclination to do evil? I remember times when I was growing up, and even later, that I would get so angry I wanted to hurt someone really bad, even my sisters. That was my natural inclination. I wanted to show them who was boss, and I wanted to be boss. Of course that is exactly the way my dad was with us and with my mom. I think he sometimes really delighted to hurt us and make us cry. The people I knew growing up were not disposed to love others. It is like they were possessed by powers beyond themselves to gain control over others. That's what sin is about and it affects us all.

Of course my dad was a fighter himself. That evidently was the way life was for him. If someone crossed him or made him mad, he hit them. We must have made him mad a lot because he hit us a lot—my mom and my sisters and me. He would say, "I need to toughen them up." I resisted the most. I believed I could handle whatever it was my father was going to do to us. Maybe that is why he hit me harder. At least I think he did.

I started kindergarten in Utah. Then we moved to Arizona. Soon we were back in Kokomo, and from there we moved to Goshen. I am not sure whether my dad was trying to keep ahead of the bill collectors if he was in some kind of trouble, or if he legitimately thought he could find work easier in a new city.

I was still in first grade when we lived in Goshen. I went to school with no shoes. The teacher sent a note home saying I needed shoes. That's when I got a pair of shoes that I really loved and that I could call my own. They had been used but I didn't care. They were mine. The problem is that I began to outgrow them and they got tighter and tighter.

Soon they were pinching my feet and hurting. My toes were curling up inside in order for me even to wear them. They were the only shoes I had. I had one shirt. It was stained and dark and scruffy.

Things didn't work out in Goshen so we moved again, this time to New York. We stayed with my Uncle John and lived in an old garage with a wood-burning stove. I don't remember anything that worked in that garage. The electricity did not work. We carried water from a pump because the plumbing did not work. I was in the second grade and school was hard. There was a girl—I forget her name—who was nice to me and helped explain things in school to me. There was a couple down the road who gave us milk. It came directly from the cow.

My dad was beating us all this time. I would go to school with a black eye or bloody lip. My dad collected buttons. He was always believing someone had messed with his buttons. "Who touched my buttons?" If someone would not confess he would beat us all. Sometimes one of us would confess so we all would not be beaten.

I sometimes thought, "Ours is not a real home." I would see how the neighbors would sit down to dinner; I would see how other people lived. We did not live like that. We did not sit down at meals. We did not eat together. When food was given to us we were expected to eat it. One time we were given peas. I did not like peas. My dad said, "You eat the peas or I'll bust your ass." I forced them down, but then I vomited. My dad was so angry he made me eat the vomit.

The whippings continued. My dad would get violent, not just to my sisters and me but also to my mom. Sometimes it was a push; sometimes it was a cuff with an open hand; sometimes he used a fist. He also let us know he had a gun. He would take it out and swing it around. It scared me. What if he had a gun in his hand when he was in one of his rages? I believe he was capable of taking a life.

The molesting had started by this time. I was only eight years old. I was miserable. The police came one day. I was afraid of my dad but I was more afraid of the police. I am not sure why but I mistrusted police. Maybe it was because of things my mom and dad would say about them. The police, two of them, knocked on the door. They said they wanted to talk with us. I was terrified and hid in a back room. They came in and found me. They wanted me to come out to the police car. There was a man and a woman. They asked about my dad. Had he ever touched me in one of those places on my body? Did he hit me? They must have known he hit me. After all, one day I went to school with a busted lip. They probably suspected the molesting.

I denied everything. They must have suspected I was lying. The male police officer said, "If my son ever lied to me I would beat him bloody." I was afraid of my dad but I was more afraid of the police. For sure, after that, the police would never get any information from me.

In the third grade we moved back to Kokomo. I was living with the horrible secret of the molesting. What the police suspected was happening, really happening, to me. Even today I have flashbacks of those times:

My dad's silhouette is at the door....He is coming in....I want to run but I cannot escape....I want to hide under the bed but I will get into trouble for not being in my bed....In my mind I am screaming...I can't scream out loud or he will beat me...I am trapped...how can I make it stop?...He tells me to get a blanket...He is lying down and pressing himself against me...He is rubbing his hand up and down my body...He is kissing on me...He is pushing his tongue into my mouth...He is rubbing me down there...He wants me to touch him...I scream to myself, "no"...Then it is over...He tells me not to say anything...He leaves.

In the flashbacks I break into a cold sweat.

I tried tricks to make it not happen. I would go and lie down with my sisters. Surely he would not do that if my sisters are there. Sometimes I would pretend to be asleep believing he would leave me if I did not respond at all. Sometimes I would say I have to go to the bathroom just to escape being with him. But it never seemed to work.

The molesting went on for months, sometimes day after day. It went on for several years. My Dad would tell me, "I have to stop. What I am doing is not good."

But it never stopped. I was so miserable inside.

One day, to make matters worse, my dad called us girls together. We sat down on the floor in front of him. He talked about touching. He wanted to know if anyone was touching us "down there." If they ever did, we were to let him know right away. I wanted to cry out, "But daddy, you are touching us." I guess I assumed if he were touching me he was touching my sisters also. "You...you...you." If it was so bad for anyone else what about our own daddy? But I was quiet.

CHAPTER 4

Angels

Our home never celebrated special days much like birthdays or Christmas when I was a kid. I don't remember that we ever had a Christmas tree, or Christmas presents, or birthday presents. Kids at school would talk about birthdays. I wondered what it would be like to live in a family where kids got presents and a cake and people gathered around and sang "Happy Birthday." Maybe I thought we were too poor, although my dad had a job. I didn't have these things thought out at the time. Maybe my dad was too stingy. There was money but it was for things like partying. What I know is that we didn't have clothes; sometimes we didn't have food. For sure my dad never spent money on us kids. We didn't do fun things.

I remember an incident from when I was in the second or third grade. My dad came in one day and said, "Hey, girls, let's go for a ride." We were excited. We had no idea where he might take us but in our minds it had to be something good. We drove through Highland Park. Kids were playing on the play equipment. They were laughing and having fun. My dad was commenting on the kids playing. I really thought he was going to park the car and let us play. But he didn't stop. He drove through the park and said, "That's what good kids get to do. It is not for kids like you."

I was crushed. My dad seemed to delight in getting our hopes up and then dashing them. One time my dad had potato chips. He asked my sister if she wanted some. She did, of course. Then he told her he didn't think he would give her one. "You can't eat just one. You'll want more." She begged for one. He gave her one. She wanted another. He answered in his know-it-all voice: "It says on the package you can't eat just one. I told you not to ask for any." She begged, but he didn't give her any more.

It was no wonder we thought fun was not for kids like us. Celebrations were not for kids like us. Treats were not for kids like us. New toys were not for kids like us. Birthdays were not for kids like us. Christmas was not for kids like us.

My dad would tell us about when he was a kid. If he beat us he would say it was nothing like the way he was beaten. If he called us names, it was nothing like the names he was called. My dad hated his mother. He was abused. He lived a horrible life. He let us know we should be happy that we didn't have it worse than what we did.

So I was alone with my feelings and my thoughts. I was learning not to trust other people. Not the kids at school. Not the teachers. Not the police. Not the neighbors. Not even my parents.

I sometimes wondered whether we—our family—were meant to be "different," not like other people. Later when I was in counseling I learned about self-worth. It is the sense that you are valuable to someone, or loved. I never had that feeling. I felt like a discarded dirty rag. My parents never cared where we were or what we did. They never called us for dinner.

In some ways we lived without hope. But in another sense I, at least, was not without hope. God put thoughts in my mind. I didn't think of it being God at the time. I just had thoughts. Now I believe God was always there, always trying to break through. I would see the stars in the sky. I would feel the grass that was soft and green. There was a rose bush in our front yard. The roses were beautiful. There was a tug, a sense. There surely was something better in the world, something more. I didn't necessarily associate it with God. But there was surely something....

One day there was a knock at the door. I had just turned ten. A man and two women wanted to talk with my mom. This was strange because people didn't often come to our house unless they were part of the partying group. This man and these women were definitely not part of my parents' partying group, or any partying group. They were different. I knew they were different. I wasn't afraid of them.

The man talked. My sisters and I watched from over on the other side of the room. The man said his name: "Ed, Ed Swain." He said they were from a church—it was Parr United Methodist Church—and they wondered if my parents would allow them to "adopt" my sisters and me for Christmas.

What did that mean?

It would be like we would be their kids for the Christmas season and they would help us celebrate Christmas. There would be a Christmas tree with lights. There would be a Christmas meal. And there would be presents.

I had this wonderful feeling. Is it possible to sense spiritual things even if you don't know anything about God or spiritual forces? I think so now, when I think back on it. I thought to myself, "angels." In my undeveloped religious world I figured this man and these women were angels. This must be what angels were like. But why us? They didn't know us.

It happened. The man and the two women found out that we needed coats and shoes. A few days later the man named Ed and one of the women came to take us to the Bargain Center on Washington Street to get coats. It was so wonderful. I had never been to a store where I could actually pick out something I wanted and then have it.

Next we went to the shoe store. I could have any shoes I wanted. I picked out some black Adidas. I was really happy. I could go to school with shoes. Other kids would talk about what they got for Christmas. I could show my shoes.

It was a wonderful Christmas. My sisters and I sat in front of the tree and just stared at it. It was so beautiful. The lights blinked on and off. We kept that tree long after Christmas. For Christmas day the people gave us food. There was a ham, and a turkey, and stuffing, and mashed potatoes, and pie. It was like more food than we had ever seen in our home.

The people who bought us the presents asked if we would like to go to their church. It was only a couple of blocks from where we lived. We went. My sisters went several Sundays and then dropped out. My mom even went once. The people from the church didn't depend on us getting there on our own. Mr. Swain would stop by and knock on the door and ask if we were going to church today. I was the only one who would go. I didn't go every

Sunday. Sometimes I was up so late, I couldn't wake up. Sometimes I wasn't interested. But something drew me. I wanted to go even when I couldn't understand what was happening. I liked the singing. I couldn't follow the sermons.

It must have been a sight—this unkempt little girl going to church with this man. Sometimes I stretched out on a pew and fell asleep. There were hardly any other kids there my age.

The church, I am convinced, really didn't know what kind of life I was living. I was smoking marijuana at the time. Actually I was dealing marijuana. I was getting it from my uncle. A guy I knew about my age named Wayne lived not far from the church. At different times I would sneak out of church and go down to Wayne's. I would sell him pot and we would smoke together. Then I would come back. I would go to the rest room and try to get rid of the smell. I didn't want the people to know what I was doing. I didn't want to disappoint them. I really liked the people. I liked Mr. Swain. It was just that, even at this age, I couldn't break away from the drugs.

Summer came and the church people told me they would like to send me to church camp. I had no idea what church camp was. The camp was Pine Creek. I went. I don't know what I was expecting. It was overwhelming. It was more than I could handle. I didn't feel right among the kids there. I was scared. I screamed that I wanted to go home. Ed came and got me.

My connection with the church went on for about a year. The second Christmas they got us stuff again. I got another pair of shoes and a new outfit—two outfits, in fact.

Eventually I was attending less and less. It was such a different world. When I attended less the contacts were fewer. I suppose it was discouraging to them. I was not appreciative. I was so irregular and then I dropped out altogether.

But the kindness stuck in my mind. Maybe I should say in my heart. I would think of the man named Ed and the women who came. And I would think "angels." Even when I was cursing and angry and stealing and hustling and doing drugs, in my heart I would sometimes think of the angels, and how maybe there really was something good in the world.

In 2010, after I was saved and on the way to recovery I had moved to Transitions House of the Kokomo Rescue Mission and got a job at Omeletty's. One day I recognized a man who came in. It was Ed, Ed Swain, the same Ed who came to my house, who bought me shoes, who picked me up for church, who took me to church camp and then came and got me when I couldn't handle it. I was so glad to see him. It was another one of the persons God put in my life. It was a reminder of a great God and how He works. It was amazing that I should run into Ed after so many years. I went up to him and asked if he remembered once taking a little girl at Christmas to get a pair of shoes. He smiled. He remembered. I'm sure he thought, "Some things you don't forget."

I shared a little about how Jesus had come into me life. He came into the restaurant more often after that and I would share more of my story. And part of the story was that even when my life was in deepest darkness, I remembered the church and the angels and they were a part of my coming to Jesus.

Ed told his pastor, Rev. B. J. Siefert, who called me and wanted to meet me. We were to meet at a restaurant. He asked how he would know me. I thought of the people who first came to call at our house and thinking they were angels. The Spirit of God was in them. I told Pastor Seifert: "I have long brown hair and you will see Jesus on my face."

I had reason to call the church. The answering machine said: "This is Parr United Methodist Church, the little church with the big heart." How awesome is that. Little church, big heart. It was a blessing.

I went to Parr. I shared my testimony in the morning worship service. I told of a lonely little girl who never had much of a Christmas and of a church that cared, and of some Adidas black shoes that I wore for years. I told of a man who came by to see if I wouldn't go to church. I told of hearing the church's motto, what was on their answering machine when I called the church, "The Little Church with the Big Heart."

And then I told about how what they did was a part of my coming to Jesus, even though all of those years they may not have known it.

And we all had a good cry and praised God.

Cynthia Burch

CHAPTER 5

It Was Tough Being Eleven

A lot of things happened to me when I was eleven years old. I grew up way too fast. I did things and knew things—or thought I knew them—that kids should never know. In other ways I did not grow up at all. I thought I could handle things happening to me, but I know now I wasn't capable of that. I couldn't understand my dad or my mom. At times I thought we might be a family. I would see other families and wish we could be like them. But we never were. We were a dysfunctional collection of needy people who didn't know how to love or even get along.

I was drinking alcohol at age two. I was smoking pot at age nine. Smoking pot came from my uncle, my dad's brother. He lived with us, more or less. Like many people I knew, he smoked pot. He would sit in our living room and pass his joint around. I would hit. I liked it. I don't think I ever tried a drug I didn't like. I began to ask for it. Then I began to think, why wait until my uncle is here. I knew where he kept the stuff. So I helped myself. He had it in a big cake, like a brick. I would just take what I wanted and smoke what I wanted. Soon I was taking a lot. There was a certain thrill in knowing you can just take something you want, use it, and feel good. It also made me feel important. I don't think he ever knew I was stealing it.

I went to school in Kokomo at Lafayette Park. Some things about school I liked. Perhaps most of all was that we got free lunches. We would not get beaten at school. But we were tormented, my sisters and I. The kids made fun of us. They called us "the dirty Burch girls." They made fun of our clothes. One day my dad trimmed my bangs. Of course he didn't know anything about trimming bangs. When he was finished they were crooked. I was embarrassed for the way I looked so I covered the bangs with a head band. There was a boy named Justin who picked on me continually. That day Justin knew I was hiding something. He tore off the headband. Kids saw the crooked bangs and laughed.

I was humiliated. Why me? Why didn't they like me? Why did they make fun of me? I was crushed. I ran to the rest room and wouldn't come out. I locked myself in. No one came to my rescue. No teacher came to help. No one asked why I was in there or if I was all right. I was there the rest of the day. At the end of the day everyone had left. I came out. My sister Carolyn was there. She, at least, had waited.

But when I had access to pot and took it to school kids paid attention. I had something no one else had. I knew about pot. I smoked pot. I might let them try it if they were nice. I even offered to sell it.

Kids bought it. Kids at school had money. They had lunch money. They had allowances. One of my best customers was a boy named Josh. He would give me $5, sometimes $10. The girls wanted pot too. I was dealing drugs at age nine. I don't think the teachers ever knew.

At home my sisters and I were getting into fights more and more. Sometimes we could play together but often our play would end in a fight. My parents never stopped a fight. One hit led to another. It was like the jungle. You hurt the other person before she hurt you. Once I stuck a fork into my sister. Once I hit her over the head. We would scream and yell and cry. My dad meanwhile would egg us on. "You better kick her a— or I'll kick yours." Once I smashed my sister's door down with a crow bar. Fights would end in blood and tears and burns and bruises. My dad would be proud of whoever dominated. Even when I lost I could not cry; that would be a sign of weakness.

It did not help that my dad seemed to favor me over my sisters. My mom liked my sisters. My dad liked me. My dad told me I was smarter than my sisters. Sometimes my sisters would do a chore and my dad would then tell me to do it over. He would say they didn't do it right. Supposedly I knew how to do it. My sisters accused me of being daddy's favorite.

My dad called me the little boy he never had. He said I was tough and mean. Is it a compliment to be told by your dad you are tough and mean? I had to be tough to live in my home. Maybe mean. I admit I was a tomboy. But I had to be a tomboy. We didn't know how to be sweet and feminine. We didn't know what it was like to wear frilly dresses. My dad would take me places—just me—like to auctions. He loved auctions. People knew him and liked him. It was good being with him but I knew that every time I went someplace with him there would be a price to pay. That for sure is when he would come to my bedroom.

He treated me differently in other ways. A few months before I turned eleven my dad met a woman named Melissa. Before this I had not thought much about my parents' unfaithfulness to each other. There were always other women around who paid attention to my dad, and other men around who paid attention to my mom, but I did not attach any significance to this.

But Melissa came into the picture and I realized the horrible truth. "Faithfulness" had no meaning in our home. One day my dad asked me if I wanted to go with him in his cab (he was driving cab at the time). I said sure. I got in the front seat. We went to Melissa's house. When Melissa got into the cab she got into the front seat with my dad and I sat in back. I knew then this was more than just a friendship.

A short time later my dad told my mom he was going someplace. Wherever he said he was going was not where he went. He picked up Melissa. Once again for some reason I was along. Why me? I never figured out the answer to that question. Why would he flaunt his unfaithfulness in front of me? We went to Indianapolis. Dad and Melissa were holding hands. I was horrified. I knew this was not good. When they got back we went to Melissa's house. They slept in the bedroom. I was on the couch.

Did my mother know about this? She must have been in denial. Surely she suspected. Anyway, I thought I had to do something. I told mom; I told her what dad was doing. She was angry—angry at me, as if I were to blame. Nevertheless, she confronted him. It made matters worse, if it were possible to be worse. He exploded. He screamed. He didn't want people telling him what to do, not his daughters, nor his wife. It was not their business. He would do what he wanted to do when he wanted to do it.

Now he was onto mom even worse. She couldn't do anything right. She was the cheater; she was the one who made things in the house worse. I tried to stick up for her. Sometimes I felt I was in the middle. But I was also feeling guilty. I was the one causing this pain. I was the one who had squealed.

From that day on things started going downhill—if it was possible to go downhill even more. Dad's anger was increasing. One day he came home yelling and cursing. He turned violent. He had a telephone cord wrapped around mom's neck. He was going to kill her. He was squeezing. She was crying and pleading. She couldn't breathe. When he loosened the cord he threw the phone at her and said he had had enough; he was leaving.

He went into the bedroom to get some things. He was serious. Of course there were times when he had left before but never after such a rage. I remember the horrible scene: my dad walking through the room, my mom begging, pleading, crying, groveling, promising things would be different. She would do anything. "What about the kids? How could he do this?" He left.

But he still wanted me. He came by the house one day and asked for me. He had a different girlfriend. He wanted me to go and live with him and his girlfriend. I didn't want to go but I didn't want to stay with my mom either. I went. I would babysit for two small children while he and his girlfriend would party.

Then one night it happened. It was Easter, 1990. The girlfriend was gone. The two small children were in the house but asleep. My dad came and wanted me to lie down with him. I didn't want to but he insisted. Before I knew it he was on top of me. This was more than just touching. He was pulling at my clothes. I tried to get him to stop but he was too strong. He had me pinned. Then he forced himself into me. It hurt so much. I screamed. It did no good. Blood was all over. I went into the bathroom afterward and tried to clean up. I felt horrible. Violated. I went home but I didn't tell my mother. I was eleven years old.

I wanted to tell someone but I could not. I couldn't tell my mother. I couldn't tell my sisters. I couldn't tell my teachers at school. I for sure could not tell any social worker that checked up on us. I was carrying around this terrible secret in my mind and in my heart.

Eventually I did tell. It was in May of 1990. I had a friend named Tina. We were playing the game "Truth or Dare." We would dare each other to do something, and if we didn't we had to tell the truth about something. Tina wouldn't do the dare so she had to answer a question. I asked if she had ever lost her virginity. She had been molested. She told me about it.

Then it was my turn. She dared me to do something. I didn't do it so she then told me I had to tell her my deepest, darkest secret. I told her I couldn't do it. "You have to, Cindy, that's the way the game is." I started crying. "Cindy, you have to tell." It was so hard but I told her what my dad had done.

"Cindy, you have to tell my mom."

"No, I would never tell."

"You have to or I will."

She practically dragged me to her mom. Her mom's name was Angela. "Mom, Cindy has something to tell you."

It came out. Then it was Tina's mom's turn to talk.

"Cindy, you have to tell your mother."

I didn't think I could do it. Tina's mom took me home. My mom was there. It was like I couldn't talk. I don't know everything I said. I must have said things that didn't make sense. I told her daddy has been touching me.

"What do you mean?"

Finally it came out that it was more than touching.

I remember mom was standing with her back to me. She had a wine glass in her hand. When I finally told her she turned and screamed and threw the wine glass against the wall. It smashed.

That's when we went to the police station. All of us, my sisters and I and my mom and Tina's mom. The police asked a lot of questions. I made a statement. They tested my sisters to see if they were virgins. It turns out two of my sisters were also being molested.

They had a court hearing. I wanted to testify but my mom wouldn't let me. I wanted to tell. I needed to tell. I wanted to be heard. But I had to be silent.

They sent my dad to prison. From that time on he was out of my life. Except he was never truly out of my life. I would see his face in my mind. When I was on the streets a man would pass and I would imagine my dad's face. When I was stripping I would look at the men and imagine my dad's face.

I did see him one other time. I was working at Taco Bell. It was six years later. I was 17. My dad was out of jail and came in. I was running the cash register. I saw him before he saw me. I asked someone else to take over the register. I couldn't even bear to look at him. I was so hurt and so angry. I did not think he was worthy of being in Taco Bell.

But because my dad wasn't in my life, at least physically, did not mean things were better. It wasn't safe at home with my dad there, but more and more it wasn't safe even when he wasn't there. My mom's life began to fall apart. Well, it was always fallen apart, but now it was even more. With my dad out of the house mom was turning more and more to drugs. Guys were coming to our house all the time. I was getting older. My body was changing. The guys began hitting on me.

One guy Wayne asked if I wanted to hang out with him. I said sure. He was 19 years old. He gave me food. He gave me drugs. He also wanted sex. I tried to resist him. I told him I would tell my mom. He said, "It ain't going to do any good. She told me I could have you." Why was my mother doing this? I felt I could not depend on anyone in the whole world. There was no one to defend me or stick up for me or protect me.

I found out Wayne was not the only one my mom told that to. She was using me for bait to get drugs or whatever she wanted.

All this time I was going to school, at least some of the time. I was missing a lot. I was floating from place to place. Sometimes I was home. Sometimes I would stay with a friend. Sometimes I was with Wayne, or, more accurately, at his parents' house. I had finally given in to him.

Sometimes I was walking the streets. Sometimes I would sleep in a closed-in porch on a glider or a reclining chair. I would leave early in the morning. People who lived in the houses never knew that someone had slept in their porch.

By the time I was 12 I was, for all practical purposes, homeless in Kokomo, Indiana.

CHAPTER 6

Friends, Who Needs Them?

I was in the fifth grade when my dad was arrested and sent to jail for molesting. It was a really bad time, both for me and for my mom. Growing up I believed my mother was the most beautiful woman in the world. She was slender with long black hair and glasses. Yet my dad always put her down. He told her she was ugly and fat. She started to drink Slim-Fast and diet even though she didn't need to. She just wanted to please him, though she never could. Nothing she ever did was good enough. He called her terrible names: *whore, slut, bitch.* She just took it. She was submissive, but not in a good way. She would not speak up for herself.

But she was dependent upon my dad. When he was gone she began acting as if she didn't care, gaining weight and doing more drugs. She stopped taking care of herself. Evidently in her mind it was better to be beaten and live with an abusive man than to be alone. She began leaning on us girls. We were all she had. But it wasn't all of us. She would dote on my sisters, but never me. I think she blamed me because I was the one who told her about dad's cheating. She was so despondent, so unreliable, so moody, and so angry; it wasn't fun to be at home.

That's when I started running the streets. I would just leave home and walk. I stayed out late at night. She never asked about me, where I was going or what I was doing. If I didn't come home she never asked where I was or what I had been doing, even if I didn't come home. It was different with my sisters. I was the odd sister out.

In the midst of all this I was going to school, sort of. I missed a lot. I was on my own. I was responsible for getting up, for getting dressed. I dressed with whatever was available; I had hardly any clothes. A couple of pairs of pants, a couple of shirts. They were usually dirty.

I went to school at Lafayette Park. It was not fun. I missed a lot of days. I was failing in my classes. I was an outsider at school. Other girls talked and giggled together and told secrets and gossiped. I didn't know what they were talking about. I thought they were talking about me. I would sit next to some of the girls at lunch but they wouldn't talk to me, so often I sat alone. I had no one that I could talk to and share secrets with. No one to giggle with. No one would come to my house just to hang out or watch TV, and no one ever invited me to go to her house.

One day in art class the teacher told us that day we were going to learn about "clash." Like many times in class, I wasn't even exactly sure what was taking place or what this was all about. The teacher said some things go together and some do not. Suddenly the teacher asked me to stand up. I wasn't sure what was happening. "Cindy, stand up." She said it again. I stood.

"Now class, look at Cindy. Look at her clothes. This is an example of 'clash.'"

I felt blood draining from my face. I was a spectacle. I was like an animal in the zoo. There were titters.

Usually I tried to be strong. Usually I would build up some defense: "They can't hurt me." But this time I was crushed, humiliated. I didn't know what to do. A few other times I had just left the room, or went to the restroom. This time I ran to the restroom and locked the door. Nothing happened. No one checked on me. No one wondered why I wasn't coming out. I didn't come out until class was over.

I don't know everything that went on in my mind while I was in the restroom but I know what I was feeling. I really was no good. I didn't know how to dress. I never heard of the idea of "clash." I didn't know what appropriate clothes were and what weren't. But even if I had I didn't have clothes to wear.

And so I learned, the hard way I guess. It was best if I stayed away from the other kids. If I got close to them I was sure to get hurt. If I sought to befriend them they would only say sarcastic things. And so people began to see me as cold and hard. I wouldn't even look people in the face. I walked around with my head down.

I believed I belonged to a different world. The people that hung out at my mom's house, I guess that was my world. It was a world of partying. It was a world of drugs. Guys were always there. Older guys. They were interested in me.

I know now they weren't interested in me as a friend. They were only interested because of what they might get from me. I could talk with these guys.

And always there were the drugs. Drugs that killed the pain, that took away the unhappiness. The best way to get the drugs was to be nice to the guys.

Did I understand all of this in the fifth grade? I am surprised now that I understood as much as I did. One way of coping was to write poems. Some months later I wrote this poem on friends.

Friends

Friends share thoughts, take care for one another,
They're there for one another
All except me, I have none.
No one to talk to, no one to see
No one to be friends with me.
No one to tell the good news or bad,
No one to tell if I'm happy or sad,
Friends, who needs them?
I don't need you.

Well, maybe I do.

—Cynthia Burch, age 13

CHAPTER 7

Living Under a Bridge

McCann Street Bridge

What happens when you cannot live at home and there is no one that wants you and you have no place to stay? The answer is that you live on the streets.

One day I was crossing the bridge at McCann Street in Kokomo. I looked under the bridge. There I saw a cement ledge that was deep and sheltered. It wasn't too dirty. I wondered if anyone even knew that ledge was there. Spring was coming and the weather was getting warmer. I crawled up in that space and went to sleep. I didn't wake up until morning. I tried it again the next night, and the night after that.

I was able to get a blanket from home. It was a quilted blanket, blue and white and knitted with yarn. It not only gave me warmth, but it was comforting. Somehow I felt more secure with that blanket. It became my sleeping bag. I left it there, along with a few other things. The bridge was becoming my "home," a place to go to when I needed to sleep or wanted to be alone. No one else seemed to know about that little special spot. Sleeping there was far better than sleeping on porches. It was also better than being at home. I wrote on the cement, "Cindy Lives Here."

I occasionally stopped back at my mom's house, usually to get some things. But I didn't stay. As far as the school was concerned I was with my mom. As far as the welfare office was concerned I was with my mom. As far as Child Protection Services was concerned I was with my mom. My mom was getting food stamps for me but she would trade those for drugs. There was hardly any food at home and there was hardly any reason for me to be there.

I was learning how to hustle, how to sweet-talk to guys to get things. I was also dealing. I knew people with drugs. I would beg from them and either use these or sell them. I could get the stuff, any of it: pills, alcohol, pot, LSD, cocaine. There was never any sense that this stuff was bad, that it could hurt me, or that I didn't know what I was doing.

It was not as desperate a situation as it might seem, or at least I thought so at the time. In fact, living under a bridge gave me a boost of self-confidence. I had always thought I was strong. I could do things on my own. I didn't need friends. I didn't need to depend on a mom that didn't seem to care for me. After I lived for a while under the bridge I thought, "I can do this."

Of course it was hard. There were problems. It wasn't always easy to find food. I could eat at school but on weekends and when summer came that was not an option. I worked the fast-food places. I would go to the counter and tell the person that they had left a cheeseburger out of my mom's order so that they'd give me one for free. I would take the food off plates after people had left.

Of course I worked the dumpsters. All kinds of food were in the dumpsters. I was smart enough to avoid the workers.

When the tomatoes got ripe tomato sandwiches became my favorite food. A tomato sandwich is a slab of tomato with mayonnaise between two slices of bread. My love for tomato sandwiches goes back to when I was in the fourth grade. I had a friend Crystal who lived next door. We played together and walked to school. She often gave me food. My mother sometimes fixed a meal at home, maybe two in a day for my three sisters and me. But we never knew for sure if we would eat, or not. Often there wasn't any food in the house, or there was food but it was locked in the refrigerator so we couldn't get it. Sometimes there was food in the house but mother was drinking, or partying, and there was no meal. We were afraid to take things out of the cupboard, or even look in the cupboard. That was off limits. If my dad knew we were snooping for food we would get yelled at, or beaten. There is much written today about childhood obesity. Obesity was never our problem.

So I was often hungry. Crystal knew I was hungry. Her mother knew I was hungry and would give me food—peanut butter sandwiches, or cookies, or soup. Sometimes if I was in Crystal's house I would ask for food. My favorite was pickles. I don't know how many times they heard, "Do you have a pickle?" One day as we played outside Crystal's mom sent out bacon-lettuce-tomato sandwiches. It was so good. I wondered how anything could taste like that. The tomato juice dripped down over my fingers and I licked them clean. Ever since that day my vision of something good to eat has been bacon-lettuce-tomato sandwiches. Crystal liked them too. We later discovered that even when we didn't have bacon or lettuce just the tomato by itself would do, provided we had some mayonnaise.

Then it stopped. The food, that is. It was related to an incident that took place just before that. Crystal and I had come home from school; my dad was in the front yard. He was mad about something. He was always mad, it seemed. If we didn't follow his rules he was mad. If he asked us to get a beer and we were slow he was mad. If we didn't answer when spoken to he was mad. And when he was mad he beat us. Sometimes it was a cuff on the head with an open hand, sometimes a hit on the behind, sometimes it was a fist. Sometimes he took off his belt. This was a belt day. He took me in the house. He hit and hit and wouldn't stop. I screamed and screamed. The next day Crystal said to me, "I'm sorry."

"About what?"

"About your getting beaten." I was embarrassed. I didn't want

Crystal to know my dad beat me. I didn't want people at school to know. I didn't want anyone to know. Maybe I thought that if people really knew I was beaten, they would think I deserved it, that I was a bad girl.

Then Crystal said her mom didn't want her hanging out with me any more. I can understand today. Crystal's mom thought I was a bad influence. She must have known it wasn't just beatings. I was cursing, drinking, doing drugs, and who knows what else, even in the fourth grade. I would still see Crystal at school, or on the way to school, and sometimes Crystal would sneak food to me. But there were no more bacon-lettuce-tomato sandwiches and no more soup.

That was just one of many times that I realized that I needed to be tough. No one was going to look out after me. I would have to do it on my own. But I figured out I didn't need Crystal to get tomato sandwiches for me. I could do that myself. I was discovering gardens. I knew several places that grew big, juicy tomatoes. I didn't think anything of taking them. I was discovering apple trees and mulberry trees and raspberries. They were down certain alleys, or in certain backyards. I tried a lot of stuff. I learned about things like green apples the hard way. No one, my mom, or anyone else, ever told me not to eat green apples because they might give me a stomach ache. Well, I got the stomach ache. The same thing happened with crabapples. I learned to eat vegetables. I was hardly particular about food. If you are hungry enough, you will eat anything.

I would pick the tomatoes, use bread I got out of the dumpsters, get a knife from McDonald's or Hardee's, along with mayonnaise packets, fix my tomato sandwiches, and sit on the grass and eat them. I loved them. It is a happy memory.

Years later, in the summer of 2010, I could have left Open Arms for the Kokomo Rescue Mission's Transitions House, but I needed a job before I moved. I applied for work at a lot of places. When jobs are in short supply it does not help when you let people know you have a prison record and you are on probation. But finally I got a job at Omeletty's, a restaurant on the west side of Kokomo. The first day there, to celebrate, I ordered a bacon-lettuce-tomato sandwich and told them to hold the bacon and the lettuce. They didn't understand. They gave me a puzzled look: "What was that again?"

"A bacon, lettuce, and tomato sandwich, and hold the bacon and the lettuce."

"You can't be serious." They thought I was joking.

"That's nothing but a tomato sandwich."

"Yeh, that's what I want."

That same summer, 2010, when I was at Transitions, I went back to visit my old home under the bridge. The little space was still there (of course—bridges don't change). It brought back a lot of memories. For one I was reminded, "I really did that." But there was another feeling I hadn't anticipated: dread. I realized how dangerous it was, a 12-year old living under a bridge. I also realized that even when under the bridge, when I thought I was strong, that I was frightened, though I didn't want to admit it at the time. The feelings came back. I was afraid of people, afraid someone would find me and hurt me. I thought about "boogiemen," which I guess were people out to get me. Sometimes when I saw men I saw the face of my father, saw him in the "boogiemen."

I realized that I was afraid of other things, more than I remembered. I was scared when it got cold, that I might not make it through the night. I would think maybe I would die. I was afraid I would not find food. I was also afraid I would not be able to find drugs—drugs that would kill the pain.

When I was under the bridge and when I was walking the streets I had a lot of time to think. I would think about other people. I wondered if anyone in the whole world lived like I did. I wondered what it would be like to live in a home where people were happy. Sometimes I would see the flowers and feel warmth and wonder if there were Something, or Someone out there. Like God.

Toward the end of that year when I was 12, when the frost came and there were no more tomatoes, I knew I could not stay all winter under the bridge. I began to look for other places to stay. Sometimes I went home. Sometimes I stayed with friends.

That's when I met Anita and more or less moved in with her. She gave me a place to stay in exchange for babysitting her kids.

CHAPTER 8

Matt – The Kids' Father

When I was 14 I was babysitting for this woman Anita who had 4 kids. Before that I was on the streets. I agreed to babysit at Anita's in exchange for a place to stay. Anita smoked and drank and took dope and partied. The kids and I would go to school while Anita worked. When she got home, she would go partying. That's when I would watch her kids. I didn't mind it. The kids and I played games. I would fix meals for her kids and me. Sometimes Anita wouldn't get home until after midnight. She took advantage of me but I was willing to do this because it was better than living under the bridge.

I was making a little money at the time with my hustling. I would sweettalk guys and they would give me money or drugs. Sometimes I would find other babysitting jobs. These were all people who needed someone to watch their kids while they partied.

I was pretty deep into drugs. I could get the stuff: pills, alcohol, pot, LSD, cocaine. At school I was an outsider. It was a different world. I didn't fit. I didn't do sports or music or dances or any of the things other girls did. My world was the drug world.

I was still in and out with my mom. I was still living with a hope that she would love me like I thought she loved my sisters. I did things for her to gain her approval, like going to the store for cigarettes, or helping clean up, or running errands.

But it wasn't working. When I went to my mom's there were often guys there. My mom was running a party house. She would flirt but she was not the main show. The main attraction was her daughters. She continually talked about her beautiful daughters. There were four of us, and more girls if my sisters had friends over. The implication was that these girls were available. All the while my mom looked out for my sisters. The two youngest were still virgins. She didn't seem to care about protecting me. She was still mad at me for turning in my dad. She knew I had had sex—with my own dad. It was not a good situation. The guys were on LSD and you could figure whatever was going through their minds wasn't good. I remember they told me I should be a stripper.

I met a girl, Nancy, at my mom's who showed me some new tricks. Get older guys to take you where they were partying. Sweet talk them into believing you were attracted to them and they could hit on you. When you were in the house look around for something to take (or steal). You could usually find drugs and sometimes money. Leave before they knew what was happening. Nancy and I would do this together. She would be my eyes and warn me if guys were coming.

One day Nancy brought Matt to my mom's. She told me she wanted me to meet this guy, Matt. Matt Bitner. Right away I felt a spark. There was an attraction there. Nothing happened at first. He was supposed to be dating my sister Carolyn.

Several weeks later Matt and Carolyn came to Anita's where I was. We all talked and I could tell I was connecting with Matt, even though he was with Carolyn. Later I went to my mom's and found Matt there with Carolyn in the room where I normally stayed when I was there. Matt and Carolyn were on the floor and he was all over her. There were others also in the room, three sleeping on the bed and two making out on the floor. I complained to my mom. "You have to get them out of there; I want to go to sleep."

When mom saw what was going on she went into a tirade. She grabbed Matt by the hair and pulled him out. After that she tried to keep Matt away from Carolyn. That's when he started chasing me. He asked if I would hang out with him. He was 18 and I was 14. Soon I was in love, or thought I was in love, as much as I knew about love. There was something huge, something magical. I started dreaming of Matt and me together. We would be a marvelous couple. We would be together forever. He was the one.

We spent more and more time at his house. He lived with his

parents, Tim and Deb Bitner. Matt's friend Nick was staying there too. So during a certain period I was sometimes at Matt's, sometimes at Anita's, sometimes at my mom's, and sometimes other places. Then, more and more I was at Matt's. I began to like his parents, Tim and Deb. They lived in an old Victorian house. It was clean, the first time I had ever stayed in a house really clean. You could eat off the floor. But they were both users. Everybody in the house was a user. Almost everybody I knew was a user.

This went on for about a year and a half. I was still in school. Eventually I got pregnant. Meanwhile my mom was threatening me. She was falling apart. Even though she didn't seem to care that much for me she wanted me around. Ever since my dad left (he was in prison at this time) she couldn't seem to take care of herself. She didn't pay her rent. She would stay one place until she got kicked out and then find another. Sometimes she was staying in places so run down she wouldn't even have my sisters there. She used money she got from welfare (she was still drawing for me) for drugs or guys or whatever. She was afraid she was going to get into trouble for the way her kids were being neglected. She threatened to turn me in if I didn't come to be with her.

So Matt and I lived with my mom for a while, at various places. One place was so awful we couldn't stand it. The woman my mom was with had maybe 40 cats and 40 dogs. It stunk. It was disgusting. I was pregnant. I started living in the basement of this house and the basement was really bad too. You couldn't eat a sandwich without a cat coming up behind your back and jumping on top of it. I mean you fought for food. The house was really, really dirty and the cats and dogs just went to the bathroom wherever. My mom and people she was with were partying all the time. Even though I was taking acid and still using it was more than I could handle.

That's when Matt and I went back to live with his parents, Tim and Deb. After where we had been it was like heaven. It had a homey feeling. And his parents really accepted me. Matt was an only child and they treated me like a member of the family. His mother and I would eat ice cream together when I was pregnant with Trent and had cravings. Our son, Trent Alan Bitner, was born on June 3, 1995. I was happy. I had someone to love, my little baby. The future looked bright. I had just turned 16. I was no longer in school. I'd been kicked out when they found out I was pregnant. I didn't care. I had a place to stay. I had food to eat.

Tim and Deb were not always easy to love. Tim was a bad alcoholic. He was mean, raging mean. Deb was a diabetic, but that didn't keep her from smoking pot. It was a horrible situation, though at the time I didn't think so. Sometimes when Tim came home drunk he was violent. He would beat on Deb. One time he hit her so hard he broke her jaw. She had to have it wired shut.

I sometimes think of those days. I think about how it could have been if we all had not been addicted to drugs. Drugs basically wiped out a whole family. Both Tim and Matt would die of overdoses. Deb would die of complications with drugs and diabetes.

In 1995 when I was with Matt the drug addiction really began to affect the way I acted and thought. On one occasion I was with my son and was high. My son was asleep in the car seat. We were partying at this friend's house. I'd had LSD, crack, pot and a bunch of other stuff. I remember looking over at my son asleep in the car seat. I was zonked. I thought that I saw blood on his face, in his ears, and on his nose and mouth and eyes. I freaked out and I was like "oh my goodness." I started screaming and yelling, crying for someone to help me. Everyone was telling me that I was seeing things but I wouldn't listen. So somebody took his car seat and went into the other room. They kept telling me I was just tripping. It took me a long time before I realized Trent wasn't bleeding; it was just that my mind was so messed up.

Shortly after that, when he was 3 months old, Trent got RSV, a respiratory virus. I had to take him to the hospital where they put him in a bubble. I couldn't hold him. I had to wear gloves and reach in. He got that virus because of all the smoke he was around, smoke from the drugs. Of course I didn't think so at the time. If he was sick it was somebody else's fault, not mine. They told me I couldn't keep smoking like that around my baby, but I wouldn't listen. I was in denial. All of this happened when I was 16 years old.

I was angry, frequently angry, when things didn't go right, but I wouldn't admit the connection between my misery and the drugs. On the contrary, drugs were what cured everything. They killed the pain, they killed the anger. I preached that drug. I loved it. The drug was everything to me. The drug was my best friend. It never hurt me, I thought. It was what I was committed to. It was the one thing that was reliable. If I was down, if I was unhappy, no matter what, the drug was the one thing that would make me feel better.

In 1997, my daughter Angel was born. I was gaining some confidence in myself. I remember thinking I would prove to everyone that I could so something. I could better myself. I even thought I should and could overcome my addiction (though I never did anything). That same year, 1997, I went to the downtown campus of the Kokomo Career Center and got my GED.

I was also working. In 1996 I worked at Taco bell; later I worked at Hill's, then Hardee's, then at Kroger. But I wasn't keeping a job. A couple of times I had to quit because I got pregnant. Usually I quit because I didn't like the rules at work, or I was too deep into drugs. I was also getting welfare. But even with my work and with welfare Matt and I couldn't pay the bills.

Furthermore, Matt and I were always fighting. He wouldn't carry his share of the load. He wasn't working. He couldn't hold down a job; he didn't even want one. He wasn't paying attention to the kids. His friends would hit on me. One guy, Ed, an African American, was there a lot. He bought drugs and partied with Matt. He wanted to have sex with me, but I kept resisting. He said, "Oh, you're faithful?" When I told him yes, he told me Matt had said it was all right if he had sex with me. There was another guy Rodney who said the same thing. I think now the guys Matt would encourage were the ones getting him drugs and he owed them something. He was willing to sacrifice me to pay a debt. Meanwhile he was unfaithful himself. I found out about this later.

When I was 19 my third child, Crystal Faith was born. Matt was gone more and more of the time. I was still living with Tim and Deb, his parents. They were, after all, the kids' grandparents. My kids began to call Tim and Deb's their home. It was the closest thing to a home they ever had. They chased the little Chihuahua. They considered it their dog. They took their first steps in that home and learned to talk in that home.

In 1988, I started dancing. Stripping. I had to find a way to take care of my kids and my home. Matt wasn't working. I wasn't getting any support. I couldn't fulfill my drug habit in ways I wanted to.

I wouldn't see Matt for long periods of time. I was still holding out that we were going to be a family. We were going to be together. The kids were going to grow up and we would have the white house with the picket fence.

Then on February 28, 2002, I got a phone call from Deb, Matt's mom. I had moved to my own apartment by this time. In a matter-of-fact voice Deb said: "Cindy, Tim's dead."

I gasped. I didn't believe it. My response was, "Why are you lying to me; what are you talking about?" Tim had overdosed. I knew people died of overdoses but I didn't think it would be Tim. He was trying to stop drinking. He had been taking antabuse, which causes a reaction to alcohol. But he had been drinking on top of antabuse which caused a fatal reaction.

It was true. He was dead. I went to pieces. Tim was the nearest thing to a father I had at that point in my life.

The Seventh Day Adventists performed the funeral at Eller's. Tim's body was cremated. Everybody was recuperating from that. I was still hopeful about Matt. He had expressed interest in getting involved in the kid's life. Deb, meanwhile, was falling apart.

Eight days after that horrible phone call, on March 8, 2002, I got another call. It was Deb again, in the same voice with the same kind of message as before. "Cindy, Matt's dead."

I couldn't breathe. A big weight was pressing down on me. It was some kind of nightmare, a bad dream. It was like I was living in another world.

I went to the house. The police, the ambulance people, and others, were there. They wouldn't let anyone in. Deb had found Matt on the same couch as Tim, laying in the same way. He too had overdosed.

I was so angry. I screamed out. Why? Why? Why? I'm not sure who all I was angry at. God maybe, though I knew very little about God. I was angry at the world and especially at Matt. Why did he do this to us? Everything in my life was going completely to pieces, although it had already been in pieces, whether I could admit it to myself or not.

So we had Matt's funeral. The same place: Ellers. The same Seventh Day Adventists. I was so messed up. I came late. I had taken twenty Xanax pills. I took Trent up to the casket. Trent had a picture of himself of the first day that he went to school. He wanted to give it to his daddy. He didn't understand why he felt the way he did. I told him his daddy went to heaven. Later on, when he would get mad at me he would tell me he wanted to go to heaven and be with his daddy, then ask where the stairs were so that he could get to heaven.

I didn't know what to say to him or how to talk to him about it. The girls didn't know how to understand it; they were so young. I couldn't deal with it. I was so angry, angry at Matt. How was he able to go, just to leave and not have to deal with these kids? How could he leave these kids with these questions?

After the funeral I did the only thing I knew to kill the pain. I went home and shot drugs.

When I lost Matt, I swore that I would never again give myself to anyone. I would never allow myself to have the same feelings for anyone that I had for Matt. I had been broken so many times by people who said nice things to me, but they didn't mean it (even though that is what I was doing to them). I wanted so much to have someone to love me. I thought Matt would be that person but it never happened. I felt so betrayed. In the end our relationship didn't mean the same to him as it did to me. He was sleeping with another girl when we were together, and even had a child by her. Worse, it didn't seem like any big deal to him.

All the time he seemed to delight in putting me down. He said awful things to me—*slut, whore*—he would curse me. Even that didn't hurt as much as when he started to deny that the kids were really his. Maybe Trent was his, but not the other two. He thought that I had been sleeping around. I believe he accused me because he wanted to justify his own unfaithfulness. He wanted to get a paternity test. So I had to go to court. It was Judge Murray's courtroom. They had to swab my kids' mouth. That just made me more and more angry. I couldn't believe he would make me do this! Of course the kids were all his. I knew that, but it hurt.

I know now I had a twisted view of love, and relationships. What I had hoped was love, wasn't. I held out onto the false hope that someday things would be better. His death brought reality to me. It would never have been better. At the time I didn't blame myself for mixed up thinking: I blamed Matt. How could I have allowed this person in my life? I felt so taken advantage of. And he wasn't even in our lives when he died. But just knowing that he was there, knowing that he was around...

I really loved him; I really loved him though maybe I shouldn't say that because I didn't know what real love was. My thinking and my feelings were so messed up by drugs. But we had these three beautiful baby children together and they loved him so much. I never spoke down on him to them because of how I felt about him. I adored him and no matter what he did.

CHAPTER 9
Stripping

"Our struggle is against the powers of this dark world and against the spiritual forces of evil in the heavenly realms."
—Eph. 6:12

I spent a great deal of my life in a dark world.

A lot of people have good feelings about school. I never did. I associate the schools I attended with darkness. School was never inviting or fulfilling; I was made fun of. I did not have any successes in school. I had a lot of failures.

Some of the houses I lived in were physically filthy and with that filth there was a spirit of despair and hopelessness. I associate all of that with darkness.

I used to walk the streets at 2:00 in the morning when I was 12 years old; while the darkness hid me from others, including cops, I was always afraid, afraid of someone or something that would "get me."

I had no good feelings about my home. I loved my mom but there were so many disappointing experiences associated with home that I couldn't even stand to stay there. I would come back at times when I had no other place to go but I didn't want to be there. It was a dark place. That is why I ended up on the streets.

During most of my life I sought out the parties, wherever they were. That was because there were drugs and alcohol at parties; they took away the pain. But I never left a party feeling loved or affirmed. Drugs put me in another world. I wanted to be there because I could not stand to live in the world as it was.

The dark world I lived in was not just physical darkness. It was also, and primarily, a spiritual darkness. God is light. To live apart from God is to live in darkness. Light is life. Darkness is death. There is no beauty in that dark world. There is no love. My mind could not function correctly in that dark world. All moral sense was gone. My understanding of right and wrong, of good and bad, was all confused. I was in spiritual bondage.

I lived in darkness but I also contributed to the darkness. I was under curses. I believe that. All my life people cursed me, starting with my own parents. They called me *bitch* and *whore* and *no good* and *dirty*. My way of fighting back was to get even, to fight against the world. I would curse back. I would curse my sisters; I would curse the guys I was staying with; I would curse the cops; I would even curse my own kids.

In the world where I was living it was probably only natural that sooner or later I would get into stripping. The guys were always hitting on me. They told me I was good-looking. Why not make something of that?

I got into stripping when I was 19. I had just had my third child, with Matt. I had always dreamed that we could have a good life together, that we would be a family.

But it wasn't working. Matt was so unreliable and selfish. He didn't pay any attention to the kids, especially the girls. He wasn't providing for us. He eventually just moved out.

That's when I took up stripping. My friend Angie had gotten a job at one of the clubs and she urged me to do it too, saying there was a lot of money in it. It wasn't hard. But it worked better if you played it smart.

We called it dancing. I don't know how serious the dancing was. It was mostly making suggestive moves and taking off clothes.

It horrifies me to think of it now though it didn't then. It was a job. It paid good money which I needed. I had three small children. My youngest, Faith, was only 3 months old when I started. I still had scars from the C-section on my body.

I had tried other jobs at fast food places but they didn't pay enough. At age 19 I had no special skills, except one: I knew how to hustle guys. I knew how to talk to them and tell them what they wanted to hear. I could pretend to live in their world. And I was good enough looking to make it work. The being smart part was never believing anything people said to you.

Even then it wasn't easy. I wasn't even old enough to enter the clubs where I was stripping. I couldn't even order a drink, at least not legally. Part of the game was that I would get guys to buy me drinks—except the drinks I got from the bar were cokes or kool-aid or colored water. I made the club a lot of money when guys paid good money for water. If I wanted to drink I would have to take it from the drinks the guys got.

I needed to drink a lot. I needed drugs a lot. Otherwise I simply couldn't do it. I felt no attraction to the guys I sweet-talked. Some were the age of my dad and I kept thinking of him. I wondered if these guys were any different. I didn't know who the guys were. They didn't give their names. Some of them looked important. Of course I never gave my real name either. We were fake people with fake names showing fake friendliness in a fake world.

Some of the men had wives and girlfriends. I'm sure they also had children. They left their families to come to the club and party and work out their sexual fantasies.

One way I could justify doing what I was doing was to think that these guys deserved to be tricked. They deserved the lies. I was happy to take their money. I wondered if it was money that should have gone to their kids.

But I was making money, good money. At times I brought home up to $1,000 a night. Some of the guys would call up the club and ask if I were working. Soon I got greedy for more and I started working two clubs at the same time, one in the afternoon and one at night.

With the money I made I was able to pay rent on the place we were staying. I could pay baby-sitters for my kids. I could buy my kids clothes and toys. But most of all, I could buy the drugs I wanted. And I wanted more and more.

I stripped for seven years. I was in most of the strip clubs in Kokomo. In one sense they were all alike. It was—and still is, I am sure—a dark, dark world.

CHAPTER 10

I Died Three Times

After I met Jesus I wanted to tell people. Of course I didn't have too many people to tell since I was in jail, and I only saw the other women a few hours each day. But I was able to tell them how God had moved in my life even when I was unaware of Him, even when (according to Ephesians 2:1) I was dead in *"transgressions and sins."* I realize now what "dead in transgressions and sins" must mean. I was dead to any awareness of God; I was dead to any real knowledge of a different way of life. I was dead to knowing of any way I could ever live that different life, even if I knew about it. I was dead to any ability to resist evil. It was as if I did not exist spiritually. I was in another world. It was Satan's world, the world of the ruler of the king of the air. Addiction is sometimes described as a disease, or a psychological disorder. But no matter how others describe it I know it is basically spiritual bondage.

But I was not only dead in trespasses and sins. I was near physical death a number of times. Matt's death haunted me. I knew if Matt could die I could die too. I was taking as much stuff as he was.

It scared me. It certainly wasn't because I thought of hell or being apart from God. God wasn't even on the radar screen at that time. I was scared because if I died it would all be over. It was weird, thinking about how I wouldn't be there to wake up the next day. But the pain in my everyday life was so great. Sometimes I wonder if deep down I didn't really want to end it all.

I don't know how many times I fell out, that is, passed out. Once it happened when I was with Robbie. I went to a friend's house where they were doing cocaine. I was also doing meth and morphine and whatever else I could get my hands on. Meth and cocaine do not go together. On this occasion this guy said, "Try this; it is really good stuff."

So I tried it. My heart started beating really hard. They wanted to take me to the hospital, but I didn't want to go because then they would know that I was using. So I started shooting up on meth thinking it would kill the pain. I felt that I couldn't get any air. I couldn't breathe. I blacked out.

Robbie tried to wake me with cold water. The drug culture wisdom was, if you fell out like that, you put the person in ice cold water, and the person would start to revive.

That time I revived but there were some other close calls. Robbie was abusive. Sometimes his anger seemed out of control. For example, he would lock me in the bedroom. He would hit me, sometimes with his fist. He would slap me. He would hold my arms. This was mostly when he was using. He would accuse me of cheating on him.

One time he tried to throw me out of a moving truck. Ironically, on that occasion we were on the way to Open Arms where my mom was staying at the time. I was going to take something to her. On the way Robbie and I were fighting. He got so angry he opened the door on my side of the truck and tried to push me out. I fought him. I don't know what would have happened if we had been on the highway. When we came to Open Arms he drove into the parking lot and yanked me out of the truck. An off-duty policeman had seen what was happening and had followed us. He pulled up behind us and got out and said to me, "You don't have to take this." Then he said, pointedly, to the both of us, "My wife and I have been married for 35 years and I have never put a hand to her."

My response was a sarcastic, "Oh sure." I guess it didn't even seem unusual to me that I was almost thrown from a moving truck. I was sure this policeman guy was lying. As far as I knew hitting and cursing and fighting were just a part of what all men and women do when they live together. I really could not imagine it being any other way.

So, because we couldn't get along and also because his place was so filthy I was sometimes with other guys. Sometimes I was with Robbie, sometimes with Scott, sometimes with a guy named Terry. It was at Terry's place that I died. That is, I physically died. I died as when the heart stops beating and the brain waves shut down and there is no breath.

It was in the latter part of 2006. I was no longer stripping; I wasn't able to strip. I couldn't handle it. Terry wasn't a boyfriend. He was a friend I did drugs with. We sold to each other, and helped each other maintain a high. But I was often with him. He would come over to where I was living, in a trailer court at the time. He had a little girl named Anna. Terry's wife had left Anna with him. I knew Terry and Anna over a period of six or seven years. Anna would come to my trailer and call me "Mommy" and stay with my kids. I told her, "I am not Mommy; I am Aunt Cindy." So she called me Aunt Cindy and she was often around.

So we, my kids and I, were back and forth, in and out of Robbie's, in and out of Terry's, in and out of Scott's. I also was sometimes with a girl named Kayly and her boyfriend, sometimes with a guy named Don, and sometimes with a girl named Bea. If this sounds confusing it is because it was. I would drag the kids to some of these places or leave them with someone. It was not the kind of life I would ever recommend to anyone.

On this one night I was at Terry's with my kids and some other people. I don't even remember who all was there. It was people I did drugs with. In some ways it was just another night. I was trying to kill the pain, trying to get away from life. I didn't know how to cope with things. I didn't know how to deal with problems, like things in my past. This stuff tormented me every day.

I needed more and more drugs. In a sense I was killing myself but I was not trying to kill myself. I just didn't care. I was afraid to die but I did't care enough to keep it from happening.

After I was there a while I went into the back room; it was like a laundry room. I was shooting up. My daughter Angel was standing outside, knocking on the door. She was nine or ten at the time. She wanted to do something. "Mommy, mommy, mommy." She wanted to go play or something. I called out; "Let me do this real quick and I'll be right back out." I remember capping the needle, then nothing. I fell out. Angel evidently kept calling for me but I did not answer.

Angel went to Terry: "My mommy is not answering me." Terry

knew I was shooting up. He said, "No, give her a minute; she'll be out." Angel went back and lay on the carpet by the door to look underneath it. She saw me on the floor. "There is something wrong with my mommy!" She was screaming. So several of them came over. They knocked. No response. They kicked the door down. I was on the floor. They checked for a pulse. There was none. Not only that, I was turning blue. They tried to move me. They thought if they could get me outdoors in the cold I might revive. It was winter. But I was dead weight. They couldn't even get me through the door.

They cleared out the needle and the fentanyl patch. They knew if they called for help and the police came they shouldn't be having the drug stuff around. Then they called 911. While the ambulance was on the way one of the guys hanging out was trying CPR on me but said there was no sign of life. No pulse. No heartbeat. I was getting cold. The ambulance finally came. They cut off my shirt and shot my heart with adrenalin. I don't know how long it was from the time I fell out until the ambulance actually got there. It was maybe 20 minutes, maybe a half hour. Maybe more. Some people when they die or are near death see shafts of light, or visions. I saw nothing. Only darkness.

The ambulance workers finally got a pulse. I don't remember that part but I do remember after they had put me on a gurney. I opened my eyes. My kids, the people hanging out, and the ambulance people were all there. Then I fell out again. The heartbeat stopped. The pulse stopped. I died again. There was a flurry of activity. They shocked me again. They got the heart beating again but they knew they needed to rush me to the hospital.

They put me in the ambulance to take me to St. Joe's. Before we got there, on the way, I fell out again. Again, no pulse, no heartbeat. I died a third time. So they went through the process again. CPR. Nothing. No movement, no pulse. More CPR. More shocks. Nothing. Nothing they tried worked. No life. I flat lined again. Finally they gave up and marked the time of death. I found out about this later because the girlfriend of a guy who was at Terry's had a scanner, and she heard the talk.

I was lying there dead. They were preparing me for the coroner. They had tried what they could and nothing worked.

I am convinced that is when God intervened. For whatever

reason God said, "I am not through with Cynthia." For some reason God wanted me alive. The blood flow began. The heart started pumping. The cold flesh was warming.

The next thing I remember I opened my eyes and there was Christy. She had married Nick, one of Matt's friends. We had stayed with them. She was in a panic. She was screaming at me: "Look at you, look at you, Cindy. You don't need to go like Matt did. Your kids need you. You can't do this."

It is terrible to say, but at the time, I wasn't impressed. I didn't care. I didn't realize the seriousness of what had just happened.

They pumped my stomach. I had methamphetamine; I had cocaine; I had heroin; I had xanax; I had oxycontin. I had everything. I took them all. I cannot explain why I didn't die except that God intervened. God "*made me alive*" (Eph. 2:5). Later he would make me alive in Christ.

But at the time? As soon as I was out of the hospital I shot up with methamphetamine.

CHAPTER 11

Persons Like Her Never Change

After Matt died in 2002 my life fell apart. That might not be quite accurate. To say "My life fell apart" assumes that it had once been together. I don't think it was ever together. There were times when it was not so bad, however. I think, for example, when I realized I really could take care of myself on the streets. I did not have to be dependent upon a mom who did not know how to love, or a father who molested me and beat me. I could do this. I could exist. I was twelve years old.

I thought I was happy when I first met Matt. I dreamed that someday we might be a family. I thought I was happy when my kids were born. I had someone to love. Of course I also thought I was happy after I first started stripping, when there was money to pay the rent and buy things for my kids and I had plenty of drugs.

But I didn't know what true happiness was, even during those times. I couldn't enjoy the beauty of the fall leaves, or the warmth of the smile of a friend. Indeed, I didn't even have a friend; that is, I didn't have anyone to confide in, or anyone I could trust. The people I called friends were people I used with or dealt with, people in the drug world. And outside of them I hardly knew anyone—maybe clerks in the store, or people who gave out assistance—but no one I could call by name that I knew personally.

Scott was in the picture starting in 2000. Even before Matt died I hung out with Scott. I met him at the strip club. He worked there. We were just friends, at least supposedly. It led eventually to our messing around but it didn't mean anything. I didn't care for him except as a person who could help get drugs, or take care of my kids. He basically moved in with me. He would baby-sit my kids while I was stripping. My kids got to know him. They called him dad. My kids got to know Scott's parents too. They called them Grandpa Joe and Grandma Betty.

Stripping meant more money and more money meant more drugs. It allowed me to branch out into all kinds of stuff: oxycontin, hydrocodene, fentanyl, Xanax, methadone, marijuana, meth, cocaine, LSD, and, of course, alcohol. Alcohol had always been in my life. It was an old reliable friend. I would mix various drugs and alcohol. I was always looking for a new high. But sometimes I was so zonked out I could hardly function, even at the strip club. Even though drugs were part of life at the club, the owners began warning me about too much. I was 26 years old.

The warnings didn't work. The more I used the more I wanted. I got irritable with the customers. I cussed some of them out. I couldn't stand to go to work. Anger was building in me until I thought I would explode. Finally I lost my job at the club. And I didn't even care. I had worked strip clubs for seven years.

Meanwhile Scott said he wanted to get out of town. The police knew him. They knew he was using. He wanted to start over. He thought Las Vegas was the place to go. We talked about going together. I was in just as much trouble in Kokomo as Scott was. If the police were after Scott, they were after me as well. Furthermore, I was scared to death of Child Protection Services (CPS). If they knew everything that was happening I stood to lose my kids.

So Scott went to Las Vegas to check things out. He called back and reported there were possibilities there. He offered to take the kids. I was so paranoid over CPS that I agreed to send them to Las Vegas. I would follow later. So that's how Scott and my kids ended up in Las Vegas without me.

With Scott gone I spent more and more time with Robbie. I had known Robbie from here and there. He was one of the guys. By this time he was also a big dealer. He dealt acid and cocaine. He was part of some ring. He would sell ten eightballs a day (worth about $2,500). He would keep the stuff in his house. I could have continued to stay with him but I missed my kids. I was calling them regularly. I thought they were safe with Scott in Vegas.

Then I lost contact with Scott. His phone was disconnected and he never called me. I began to panic. I was in Kokomo. My kids were in Las Vegas with a guy I didn't even consider a boyfriend. My paranoia kicked in. I imagined all kinds of things. I had never trusted anyone; why would I trust Scott? If everybody was out to get me, why not Scott? I thought of child prostitution. The word kidnapping was in my mind.

So, I was able to scrape some money together and head for Las Vegas. I didn't even know where Scott was in Las Vegas. I did have the address of the gas station where he had first worked when he went there. The people there knew him and told me he was in a certain apartment building. By this time my anger and my paranoia were consuming me. I called the police. I told them this guy had taken my kids. Maybe he was kidnapping them. The police came with me when I went to the building where Scott was. I stayed back while they went to the door of the apartment.

The police were able to speak with Scott. Scott then asked if he could speak with me. The police officer came to me and asked if that was all right. I said sarcastically, "Sure, he is really good at talking." But I spoke with him. My fears were unfounded. Scott meant no harm. He had not called because the phone had been disconnected. He was not happy that I had accused him. The kids were at school but he would get them when school was out and bring them to me. When they were on the way home from school he told the kids he had a surprise for them. My daughter asked if the surprise was a dog. Scott told them to put their hands over their eyes. When they came in the door Angel said, "I know that smell, that's my mommy." There was a moment of joy. My daughter knew me by my smell.

But Scott, and now I, and my kids, were in trouble. He had no job and no money. The kids were in school but he wasn't able to take care of them. He would be happy if I took them off his hands. But of course I couldn't. I had no place to go and I had no means of support. Scott's apartment was unfit to live in. There was no food. There was filth everywhere. The one bathroom was down the hall that we shared with other apartments. Part of the building was rented to a tattoo place.

So Kokomo didn't seem so bad. But how to get back? Scott was now into cocaine. We would soon be kicked out of the apartment because he wasn't paying rent.

Scott's parents came to the rescue. They would send Scott money to get back to Kokomo. Not only that, they would send money for the kids.

What about me?

No money for me. Scott's parents cared enough for the children that they wanted them to be cared for. But they would just as soon care for them without me. They didn't think I was a fit mother, either in Vegas or in Kokomo. In addition I was a bad influence on their son who already had enough problems. As far as they were concerned I could stay in Vegas. So Scott and my kids took the plane back to Kokomo and I was left alone in Las Vegas. By this time my return ticket to Kokomo had expired.

If this sounds mixed up and confusing it is because it was. At first Scott and my kids were in Las Vegas when I was in Kokomo. But now Scott and my kids were in Kokomo while I was in Vegas. I found out later there were shelters in Vegas where I could have taken the kids but I was too bummed even to take the initiative to seek help.

So I was on the streets in Las Vegas. By this time I had discovered ice—it is a form of meth. It is more powerful than the meth we cooked in Kokomo. I went through a horrible several weeks. In Las Vegas I knew no one, not even the people in the drug world. I was begging for drugs. I was begging for food. I had no place to stay, not even a bridge like I had in Kokomo. Vegas was a hard, cruel place. If there was help there I didn't know how to find it. Vegas was full of the homeless. They would sleep in boxes. They would attach a tarp to the side of a building and that would be their home.

Drugs were all over. When I got access to some drugs I would take so much I would just fall out wherever I was. It was cold in Vegas, at least at that time of the year. I couldn't stand to be outside but I was not welcome in any place inside. In Kokomo I knew people I could sometimes stay with. Not so with Las Vegas. I sometimes tried to hang out in the casinos. I would pretend I was playing the slot machines. I would even hang out in the restrooms. But I was so unclean and unkempt and the casinos policed the places so well that I was always thrown out. Sometimes, though, even an hour in a restroom would help me warm up before I faced the cold.

I trusted no one. I didn't have enough self-confidence even to carry on an intelligent conversation with people. I didn't have enough self-confidence to apply for a job. I once had done stripping but I couldn't even do that. I was so dirty. One time I was walking and a big limousine pulled up. The window opened and a guy looked out. He spoke to someone in the back seat: "How about this one?" The answer came back, which I heard, "No, she's too dirty." I wasn't even fit to be a prostitute.

I hung out around the apartment building where Scott had lived. One reason I hung out there was that I knew the restroom upstairs that went with the apartment Scott had lived in was not locked. At least I had access to a restroom. I also knew the corners in the halls in that building where I could curl up and sleep for a while. Otherwise, I just walked the streets. I was desperate for food. I was sitting on the grass one day and a person came up and gave me money for a sandwich. I still remember how good that sandwich tasted. But I could not depend on handouts.

I am convinced now if I had had to be in that situation much longer I would be dead. I began to lose even the will to live.

Only later did I realize that I was not abandoned. The great Good Shepherd was seeking me out. When it seemed that all was helpless, God put the right people on my path. One day I saw several people cleaning up the empty store front on the street where I was hanging out. A man there spoke to me as I passed on the sidewalk. He said, "You'd better slow down."

What a strange thing to say. I knew what he meant. He knew I was on drugs. It is interesting because it was a black man who spoke to me. My father hated blacks. I once had a Barbie doll that was black. My dad found it and flew into a rage. "We ain't having any——babies here," and threw the Barbie doll into the trash. Another time I had gone with him to a place and I knew the kid in the house next door. He was a black kid from school. I was talking with him when my dad found us. He dragged me by the hair, and said something like, "Get away from that——. I don't want my kids talking with any——." Despite all my feelings about my dad, he still influenced me. I wasn't sure about black people.

I think God was teaching me a lesson. The people who rescued me in Vegas were primarily black Christians. The place that was being fixed up was going to be a new drop-in location for Narcotics

Anonymous (NA). The people cleaning the place were former addicts who wanted to help people. They started talking to me. I had no place else to go so I began to hang out there. People there sensed how bad-off I was. A woman told me if I wanted a shower I could go upstairs to a shower. It was the first shower I had had in maybe a week and a half. She gave me clean clothes; they were her clothes she had brought from home.

A man offered to take me home with him so I would have a place to stay. I slept on the couch. He gave me supper. He was black. The next night I went home with a woman. I stayed there two nights. I began to share my predicament. My kids were in Kokomo. I had no way to get there. My round-trip ticket had expired.

The folks at the NA center were able to get my ticket updated. I could come back to Kokomo! Furthermore, while I was with the NA people I had not had any drugs, at least for about two days.

In some ways two days without drugs was helping to restore my sanity. But in another way I was miserable. I was suffering withdrawal. I got on the plane. Robbie met me in Indianapolis. We came back to Kokomo and went to his place. My addiction overpowered any thoughts I might have had about coming clean. I shot up. My period of being without drugs lasted less than 48 hours.

The next day Robbie took me to see my kids. They were with Scott's mother. The house was clean. It was a joy to see them and be with them. That joy, however, soon turned to despair. On Christmas Day, 2004, I was at Scott's parent's house. The kids were there. I was giving my girls a bath. Angel said, "I have to tell you something." I said "What?"

Angel looked at Faith. "Faith, if you don't tell her, I'm going to." I asked, "What?"

"My dad is abusing me."

All the terrible thoughts of the past came rushing up. I thought I would vomit. She considered Scott her dad. He was there since she was a baby. The guy I thought cared for my kids was molesting. I thought I would explode. I needed to get my kids out.

I took them to Robbie's. I knew Robbie's house wasn't the best place, but I didn't know what else to do. It was Christmas break. I needed to tell somebody what was happening to my kids. As soon as Christmas break was over I called the school. It was difficult for me to do things like this but it involved my kids. My anger propelled me. I also called Child Protection Services (CPS). They needed to know about the sexual abuse. The school social worker agreed to talk to Angel and Faith. The woman at CPS, Teresa Bird, said they would be involved. Teresa Bird already knew me because she had visited places I was staying several times to see if I was fit to have the children. She had searched places I had been to get something on me but never found stuff like drugs. I had to cooperate with the school and CPS because if I didn't it could be used against me if the issue of keeping the kids came up.

So they talked with the girls. Afterwards my daughter came home from school and talked with me. "Mommy I don't want to talk to them."

I said, "Why?"

She said, "Because they want me to talk about you and tell them that you're a bad mommy."

In the end nothing ever came out of whatever investigation they did about the abuse. Nothing. When I needed help it wasn't there. The abuse went unpunished and I just got myself in more trouble. My anger was building and building, even when it seemed it could get no worse.

I talked to a police officer for the D.A.R.E. program, Jeff McKay. He had worked with me because he knew I was in addiction. He had helped me out with the kids for Christmas. I told him about Faith being abused and nothing had been done about it. His advice, "At least you have the kids out. Let it go." So there was no help even there.

So if I had had paranoia about the police and the authorities before, it was getting even worse. My living situation was also getting worse. My relationship with Robbie was breaking down, though it had never been one of love. I was now under suspicion. The police started coming in and out of the house like crazy. One day they came and busted the door in and put guns to the kids' heads and told them to get on the floor now. They searched through the house but they didn't find anything. But they told me that the house was unfit and that the kids would have to go. The kids were freaking out, saying, "I'm not leaving mommy, I'm not leaving mommy."

The police wanted me to get my kids out of the house immediately. Was there anyplace I could go, even for just a little bit? I thought of my grandmother (my mother's mom). Down through the years she was never any help. Maybe now.

I said I would take the kids to my grandmother's. It would at least get the police to leave me alone until I could figure something out. So they took me and the kids to my grandmother's. I said, "Grandma, let them stay here for just an hour and then I'll be back." She didn't even want to keep them for an hour. I pled. Finally she relented. "Well hurry up!"

I still had no place to go, but the police were gone. I came back and picked up my kids. But we were homeless. Surely they—the police, the Child Protection Services, the school—people out to get me, were watching me. So for a while we were living night to night at different places. During the day we were just sitting out on the grass, wondering where we were going to go. At nights we just walked around in the cold. The kids would cry: "It's so cold mommy. I just want to stop."

And I would get so mad. "You can't stop. We have to get there." I would cuss my own kids.

I had no inkling about how to be a mother. I loved them. I STILL love my kids. But I didn't know how to do the things mothers are supposed to do. My addiction was so bad, I couldn't think straight. Worse, I didn't care. In January of 2007 the police and people from CPS came to the house I had finally been able to rent. Any money I had was coming from the social security that I was receiving after Matt's death. Once again, as before, the place where I was staying was not fit. Sewage was backing up. There were baggies and residue of dope. I told the police that they could give me a drug test; at that moment I was clean enough to pass. I wasn't clean clean; it was just that I had not used enough at that moment to fail the test. I was taking methadone, the prescription drug I was given.

So once again I was told I had to move the kids from an unfit house. So once more I told them I would move them. Now where? To my sister Loretta's. I had just briefly contacted Loretta. They called Loretta. Loretta didn't really want to, but said she would. I had been arrested so I would be going to jail. Loretta could keep the kids until I got out of jail; then I could get them back.

I went to jail for two weeks. They discovered I had lice. My kids had it too. They were treating my head and it was really bad. When I got out of jail, I was able to see my kids, but I was not supposed to be at the same place they were until I was clean. But there was no way I could get clean.

This all seems like a terrible nightmare now. More darkness. More confusion. Satan is known as the prince of the power of the air. I was surely living in his domain. Nothing I tried worked. When I got out of jail and went to my sister Loretta's I found that she was addicted to internet porn. Furthermore, there was not a good situation with Loretta's husband. He was weird. For one, he was hitting on me. Not only that: he was treating one of my daughters differently from the other one. He called her special. He took her places. I was paranoid about molesting. Loretta's place was as bad or worse than all the other places that I had stayed. The dog was pooping everywhere and no one was cleaning it up.

So I came to take the kids to move them once again. Loretta's husband didn't want them to leave. I had to. But where now would I go?

I tried Terry's, another guy I knew. It was at Terry's that I had overdosed and died. He was still using and there was no way CPS would allow Terry to be around my kids. Finally I was so tired and so beat-down, I was ready to give up. I had no more resources. I had no more energy. I called Mike Deardorff of Child Protection Services. They came and took the kids to foster homes.

I was still able to see the kids but it was at the Villages, a place connected with foster care. Whenever I saw them people were in the room watching me like a hawk, taking notes. I felt like a criminal. They were suspicious. It was like they were trying to figure out ways that I was unfit. I was so angry. They knew I was using. I would scream at them. I hated them. I tried to avoid them, not talk with them. But I was trapped. I was supposed to be clean in order to see my kids and it was impossible for me to be clean. I could never pass a test.

September 27 of 2007, was the last time I saw the kids. I felt I was dead. I might have committed suicide but I did not even have the strength to do that. Drugs were my only escape. I couldn't face any new day without drugs. I remember sitting with my arm tied up and the blood flowing, sore all over. It was so bad I couldn't find a place to put in the needle. My arm would swell up because I would miss the veins. It wasn't just meth; it was anything and everything.

I was mixing everything. I was cooking methamphetamine. I got acquainted with people who were big-time dealers. In exchange for drugs they sometimes used me as a driver. One time I drove for a man who had been ripped off in a drug deal. He wanted me to go to a house. He told me, "They'll let you in. Just get in the door." I didn't care. He had guns to those people's heads.

At Christmas I wanted so much to see my kids. I called CPS to see if it was possible. Not if I wasn't clean. I wasn't. They told me Trent had told them he had been abandoned like a dog. I wept.

I used to tell my kids that we were concrete. You go through life and you see these concrete pillars that hold buildings up and together. That's what we were like: concrete pillars. A storm will come by and it will maybe put a crack in the pillar or cause dust, but no matter what, because it is concrete it will stand. We—my kids and I—were concrete. We were together.

My daughter wrote in the letter that I got for Mother's Day when she was in foster care: "You said that we were concrete, but you lied. Something came between us. The drugs came between us. The drugs are the reason that we don't have you." She said, "I am tired of that cycle. I am just plain tired." She was eleven years old.

Later, after my conversion, when I was in jail, I went to court. A decision was going to be made about custody of my kids. I was cuffed and shackled, but I was hopeful. My life had changed. I had been converted. Surely that would count for something. Surely when I got out of jail I could have my kids.

Joshua Light was the prosecutor. CPS gave testimony. It was a terrible, crushing blow. They really didn't believe my conversion. They didn't believe I would ever be any different. I remember the words:

People in Cynthia's circumstances will not be different. Persons like her never change.

It was like a nail in a coffin. It was a judgment of death.

But by that time I knew they were wrong. They had not taken

into account the power of God.

CHAPTER 12

Wounded Healers

I had sunk to the bottom of bottoms. I had nothing left, in body, mind, and spirit. I was totally wasted. I was a living zombie. I was a slave to meth. It was not just the meth that possessed me. It was what was behind the meth: principalities and powers, the evil designs of the evil one, the world rulers of the present darkness. I belonged to that dark world. The drug and those evil powers had become my god. I had my own names for my god: *The Girl, Bitch, Crystal, My Girl Friend*. I had sold my body for that god. I had taken cursing and abuse for it. I lied for it. I stole for it. I lost my children because of it. I had thought I was strong, but I was not. I thought I could control my life, but I could not. The drug—and Satan—owned me. And there was nothing left.

The date was April 13, 2008. Despite the darkness of that day, I look on it as the beginning of my journey out of bondage.

I was living with Robbie and Robbie's brother, Curt, at 2116 N. Delphos. I called Robbie my boyfriend, at least at that time. Maybe he was just another man. Even with Robbie I would run off with other guys. There was no sense of faithfulness or loyalty. Still, I had lived with Robbie five years. Why? The meth: the god we served in common.

When Robbie was young he had bitten into an electric cord and had been badly burned. He went through a series of surgeries. He was told he would never be able to work. There was one kind of work he could do—cook meth. He did meth. He did cocaine. He did a lot of things. He said he loved me. But he was controlling.

He did not want me even to leave the house. We could not work together, even cooking meth. We worked independently. He needed me. Maybe I needed him.

The house where we stayed personified the darkness I knew had settled over me. There was no beauty there. The house was so dirty there were maggots under the rug. We could not walk barefooted because our feet would be black. We could see through the cracks in the walls to the outside. Like our own lives, it was full of filth. There was always a stench. The stench was from anhydrous ammonia, and Martin's drain cleaner, and lithium battery strips—all chemicals we used to cook meth.

From time to time I would think I needed to clean the house. I would open up the windows just to let fresh air in. But it never worked. The stench was still there…and the dirt… and the darkness…and the hopelessness…and the god we served.

I guess God needs us to be broken before we are willing to listen to Him. On that day I was broken. I had been broken many times, but this time I was totally broken. Was there any reason to live? Then, on that day, April 13, 2008, late in the afternoon, God put into my mind a reason to live. I happened to look up on the wall, and I saw my children's pictures: Trent, Angel and Crystal Faith. They were school pictures of several years ago. The children were smiling.

I wept. What had happened to me? I missed them so very much. Something had destroyed my relationship with my own children. It was meth, and more. It was my attitude, my anger, the life I was living. I would not have described it so then, but it was the Evil One, to whom I had become enslaved.

I kept weeping. I wailed. In my misery God came into my mind, and I fell to my knees. I had never fallen to my knees before. I had prayed before, for help to get out of the messes I was in, to escape trouble, to be happy.

But this time was different.

"God, help me. Please help me. Oh God, help me. I can't make it. Please God."

I didn't know much about faith. I did not have the faith that could move mountains. I did not have the faith that could move even a shovelful of dirt or even a few grains of sand. But I must have had the faith of a mustard seed. The tiniest seed. A tiny bit of faith, but with that little bit of faith I cried to God. A mustard seed faith. And God heard my cry. I can't describe it well, but in that moment God was in the room.

That moment of sensing God's presence passed, but it was enough. God was going to show mighty power. But how? Is it possible even to conceive of a series of events that could lead me out of bondage? It is most unlikely.

I needed to get out of the house. The oppressive darkness of the place was overbearing. I needed to be able to breathe. I had an excuse. I needed to deliver some meth. I took a shot of meth to fortify myself. Little did I know that would be the last shot of meth I would ever take.

I slipped out of the house and walked down Delphos Street in Kokomo to Morgan and turned west. It was early evening. Dusk. A police car drove by and slowed.

Fear…anger…panic. I was paranoid about police. For years, even as a little girl, and as an adolescent, and as an adult, I hated police. They were always out to get me. They would be chasing me. I would have hallucinations about police being on the roof of the house. One night I went up on the roof to look for them. I was sure they were hiding all around, watching me. I would send Robbie to look for them. Robbie would get so mad. "There is no one here," he would say but would go just to prove to me they weren't there. I began to believe everyone was police. So I wouldn't talk with people. I thought my house was bugged with cameras or bugging devices. I thought police were under the floor boards. I would sometimes hide my stuff, my meth stuff, so police wouldn't find it. One night it was so bad I took off running down the street. Robbie chased me. I was yelling at him to get away. Police were bad news. They would question me. How many times had I been picked up?

Does God have a sense of humor? I hated police so much and yet the first person God sent on my path to deliverance was a policeman. The police car slowed and turned around and came back and stopped. Normally when I saw a police car I faded into the shadows or slipped down an alley, but not this time. Something, or Someone, made me hesitate.

There were two officers. They rolled down the window and asked my name. What was I doing? There was still time to run—

or to lie. I could make up a story; give my sister's name or someone else's. It turns out they weren't even looking for me. Despite my paranoia they weren't even suspicious of me. They were checking me out because they were looking for someone else. I could have escaped by lying. But for once I gave my name, my real name.

"Cindy Burch."

God must have been in my mouth.

They ran a check. My name kicked out. There was a warrant out for my arrest: violating probation, and probably some other stuff. They confronted me. They searched me and found the meth I was going to deliver. That was all they needed. The routine began. Like an old record. Degrading handcuffs...a ride to the police station...booking. More questions. Whom had I seen? Where was I going? Where did I get the stuff? Where had I just come from? I responded in my usual way. If God was helping me through all of this I surely wasn't going to make it easy. I made up stories. I was good at it. Stories on the spot. I could think of marvelous stories. I wasn't doing anything...I was going to the store... I was just out for a walk. I lied. I fought back: why were they were out to get me? I screamed. I cursed. I hated them. I accused them of hating me. Why couldn't they leave me alone?

On August 24, 2010, I had gotten off work. My friend Tim had picked me up. I wanted to relax from the day. We drove to the park and looked at the stars and thanked God. And we danced. On the way home we were stopped by a policeman. It was in front of the Kokomo Rescue Mission. The officer knew Tim.

"Hello, Tim. I pulled you over because you have a plate light out." Tim thanked him.

Then the officer looked at me. With a puzzled face he asked me my name.

"Cynthia Burch. I have my ID if you want to see it."

Then he said, "I know who you are. Didn't I pick you up on Morgan Street a while back?"

I remembered also. He was the one. He was the one who stopped me and questioned me and then booked me. A little while ago? It had been two years and four months before. How had he remembered? After I had cried out to God for help, and walked into the dusk of the evening, he was the policeman that had stopped me. He was the one who cuffed me and took me to the station.

How awesome, that I should meet the man again! I had hated him at the time but it was God's doing.

He said to me, "You are so different."

I said something that must have seemed strange to him. "Do you know you saved my life?'

He gave his line again, "You look so different."

"I know, I was a mess then."

"Yes you were.........but now you look so different."

I told him how long I had been in the Drug Court Program and how long I had been clean. I told him of Laura my probation officer and Judge Menges and how I had found new life.

"You look so different." (I began to wonder if that was the only thing he could say.)

"Thanks for saving my life."

He told me to continue to do good.

What an amazing experience, that God would place people back in my life so that I could thank them. And so I can be reminded that it all came from God.

Later when a woman accompanied me to the changing room to put on my jail uniform a Kroger bag fell out of my pants. In it were separate bags of meth. They hadn't found all the drugs. I tried to hide the bag but the attendant saw it. I cursed. Now I would be charged with dealing. "Please let me throw it away, I'll offer you money." "Please." I begged her. She could not do that, she said. So I was back for more questioning.

What was in the bags? The stuff was in coffee filters, which we used to drain away the water. They guessed: cocaine, crack, heroin, meth. "Do you want to tell on anybody?" They always asked that question, as if I would ever tell them anything.

"I don't know of nobody." "I just found it."

"Why are there different bags?"

Are they dumb or what? I gave a smart answer. "They're different flavors for different people."

My booking obviously was not going well. The grilling and the booking and the waiting took three hours. I was my usual angry self the whole time.

They finally put me in the holding cell or drunk tank. My body was screaming for more meth. I went into convulsions. It was like demons possessing me. They were working through the meth. They were calling out for my soul. I felt that they would kill me if they could. The people at the jail thought I was suffering from an overdose.

Overdose? Of course. All my life was an overdose.

They figured out what to do: send her to Howard hospital and get her stomach pumped.

In the hospital I was in and out of consciousness. A drug stupor. A nurse was speaking. I'm sure she did not think I was aware of her words. But I was. As they were preparing me for pumping my stomach, she spoke. I don't know to whom she was speaking. Someone with her I guess. It was a judgment. A judgment I didn't want to hear.

"Do you know this girl is only 29. She looks like an 80-year old woman."

It was true. It was the horrible truth. Even I could hardly stand to look at my face in the mirror. It was drawn and haggard. I weighed less than 100 pounds and had open sores over my whole body, from the top of my head to the bottom of my feet. My hair was straggly. My face was ashen, like a ghost. There were scratches where I had tried to relieve the itches brought on by meth. My teeth were rotted into my gums. My arms were black and blue from being shot up. I was a 29-year old that looked like an 80-year old woman.

They put a tube in my mouth that was supposed to go to my stomach. They wanted me to swallow but I was refusing. They couldn't get it to work. They were yelling because I was not cooperating. A nurse said, "Don't fight this or we'll put the tube through your nose." For being on a drug high the whole experience is still clear to me. They forced the smaller tube through the nose. I screamed. The tube hit my lungs. I couldn't breathe. I thought

I would die. They pulled it out. It was bloody. I vomited—all over my clothes, my jail clothes. I finally cooperated just to get it over with. They put charcoal through the tube into my stomach. I was hooked up like I was on life support. Perhaps I was. I had a heart monitor and an intravenous tube; my blood pressure was dropping so they were giving me medication for that; my potassium level was low; I was on a catheter.

There was not much there, in the stomach. If there was an overdose it was not in my stomach. It was all through my body, in my blood, my muscles, my brain, my arms, my legs.

When it was over I was not to eat for three days. I was already so thin my bones were showing through my skin. I got my own personal guards: male guards on twenty-four hours a day. I was handcuffed and chained to the bed. I guess they thought I was dangerous. Either that or they thought someone would sneak drugs in. Or they thought I would escape; or maybe they needed to keep me from visitors. I didn't leave the bed for three days. Bowel movement? No. There was nothing to move. The three days were spent sleeping, tossing, fighting sickness, and coming in and out of a drug stupor. The poison was seeping out of my body. Withdrawal would take months but it was beginning.

In a sense I was thankful for the guards because at least someone was in the room. Maybe I was important enough to watch.

At the end of the three days they were ready to send me back to the jail. I was given back my uniform, the one I was wearing when I came. It was stained from the vomit and still reeked.

Then a kind thing happened. In a world where everything goes wrong a kind thing is remembered. Officer Hattion—I remember his name—was to accompany me. He saw the uniform and declared that I should not have to wear a vomit-stained uniform. He called the jail: send over a clean uniform. Someone replied she already had her uniform for the week. She can make do with it, they said. But he was even more persistent. "I refuse to make this girl wear this uniform back to the jail. She is here and I am here until the uniform comes." The clean uniform was delivered.

God was putting the right people on my path. I was astounded that someone thought I had at least enough value to deserve a clean uniform. I needed every small bit of encouragement.

Back at the jail I was put in solitary confinement for a day; then I was put in a cell. It was familiar territory. I had been there before. Four different times I had been in jail. Always before I fought it: I would curse: at the steel doors, at the concrete. I would curse the people who put me there. I would curse the world and then I would scheme about what I would do when I got out.

But this time was different. Maybe I was too broken or maybe too sick. Maybe God was working. I just lay on my bunk. I had two cellmates—Rachel and Terri—but I said nothing. I was tossing and turning. I was miserable. I didn't want cellmates. I didn't want anything. I vomited repeatedly. I sweated and then had hot and cold chills. I hurt all over. This went on for the rest of the day and that night.

The next morning it happened. An amazing thing happened.

Evidently I was in the right place at the right time with the right person in the cell with me. God must have said, "OK, time to roll."

The silence was broken with words, spoken words, strange words. It was like a voice from heaven. It was my cellmate Rachel's voice, speaking God's words. Who were the words for? What were they about? Actually Rachel was speaking the words for herself except I know God was intending them for me, though I didn't know so at the time.

> *"…take your stand against the devil's schemes. For our struggle is not against flesh and blood, but against the rulers, against the authorities, against the powers of this dark world and against the spiritual forces of evil in the heavenly realms…finally, be strong in the Lord and in his mighty power. Put on the full armor of God so that you can take your stand against the devil's schemes."*
>
> —Eph. 6:11, 12

Rachel was reading from the Bible. I wasn't even sure at first what it was, and when I found out I was not particularly pleased. I didn't feel like I wanted anyone to talk to me, let alone read from the Bible. Rachel read the whole passage. I tried to put it out of my mind. But the words were forcing themselves into my head: *powers of this dark world, and the devil's evil schemes…*

I don't remember much else from that day except for more misery. Pain racked my body causing me to toss and turn. I just could not get comfortable. Withdrawal.

The next morning God was back. The silence was broken with the same voice. The same voice said the same words. Rachel was reading again. She was reading the same passage.

"What in the "s#%@s*#*" was this all about?"

> *"...take your stand against the devil's schemes. For our struggle is not against flesh and blood, but against the rulers, against the authorities, against the powers of this dark world and against the spiritual forces of evil in the heavenly realms...finally, be strong in the Lord and in his mighty power. Put on the full armor of God so that you can take your stand against the devil's schemes."*
>
> —Eph. 6:11, 12

What was happening? This was annoying. I tried to put the words out of my mind except they stayed there: *our struggle is not against flesh and blood.* The miserable symptoms of withdrawal continued throughout that day.

The next morning God was back. On the third day the silence was broken with the same voice saying the same words.

> *"...take your stand against the devil's schemes. For our struggle is not against flesh and blood, but against the rulers, against the authorities, against the powers of this dark world and against the spiritual forces of evil in the heavenly realms...finally, be strong in the Lord and in his mighty power. Put on the full armor of God so that you can take your stand against the devil's schemes."*
>
> —Eph. 6:11, 12

By this time God was beginning to get my attention. Certainly Rachel was getting my attention, even if she did not know she was reading for me.

"Evil powers?" "The devil?" What is this? I asked Rachel. I asked several of the women in the unit. I don't remember what they said. I continued throughout the day to battle the savage effects of withdrawal.

The next morning God was back. The fourth day, the fourth morning. Rachel again. The same voice and the same words. Was this a broken record?

> *"...take your stand against the devil's schemes. For our struggle is not against flesh and blood, but against the rulers, against the authorities, against the powers of this dark world and against the spiritual forces of evil in the heavenly realms...finally, be strong in the Lord and in his mighty power. Put on the full armor of God so that you can take your stand against the devil's schemes."*
>
> —Eph. 6:11, 12

Something came to my mind. I remembered once years before that my mother told me I was filled with the devil. It always stuck with me. Now my cellmate is reading to me about the devil? What were the powers of this dark world?

By this time I was talking about it on the unit, not just about that passage but about the Bible. The women were responding to my questions. This was unusual. This was *totally* unusual. Jail is a jungle. People who go to church and are religious talk about the Bible, not women in jail. But here I was in jail talking to women about the Bible. One of them was Missy Lee. God must have put Missy Lee on that unit just for my benefit. Missy Lee told me the Bible was God's Word.

The next morning God was back. The fifth day, the fifth morning. Rachel again. The same voice and the same words.

> *"...take your stand against the devil's schemes. For our struggle is not against flesh and blood, but against the rulers, against the authorities, against the powers of this dark world and against the spiritual forces of evil in the heavenly realms...finally, be strong in the Lord and in his mighty power. Put on the full armor of God so that you can take your stand against the devil's schemes."*
>
> —Eph. 6:11, 12

How awesome! My heart was suddenly hungry for more, and more, and more. I kept asking more questions. What is this Bible? What is God's Word? Several women had Bibles. They let me look at them; Chaplain Green got me a New Testament to use. I remember it was the King James Version and it was hard to understand. Still I understood enough to realize that Paul, who talked about taking the stand against the devil's schemes, was probably writing from prison, just like me. People studying these words were in jail, just like me.

All of this was happened when I was physically miserable. Withdrawal is a horrible thing. I felt sick all over. I was too sick to want to do anything. Yet in spite of this I had this attraction for the Bible.

The next morning God was back again. The sixth day, the sixth morning. The same voice, the same passage.

> *"...take your stand against the devil's schemes. For our struggle is not against flesh and blood, but against the rulers, against the authorities, against the powers of this dark world and against the spiritual forces of evil in the heavenly realms...finally, be strong in the Lord and in his mighty power. Put on the full armor of God so that you can take your stand against the devil's schemes."*
>
> —Eph. 6:11, 12

The next morning God was back again. The seventh day, the seventh morning. The same voice, the same passage.

> *"...take your stand against the devil's schemes. For our struggle is not against flesh and blood, but against the rulers, against the authorities, against the powers of this dark world and against the spiritual forces of evil in the heavenly realms...finally, be strong in the Lord and in his mighty power. Put on the full armor of God so that you can take your stand against the devil's schemes."*
>
> —Eph. 6:11, 12

This could not be an accident! God was speaking to me! God was speaking about the armor of God and the Devil's evil schemes. It wasn't too hard to figure out. My addiction and the devil's evil schemes—they were the same! Truth was knocking at my heart's door. Months later I read that Joshua's army walked around the walls of Jericho seven days, and on the seventh day the walls crumbled. Rachel read the "devil's schemes" passage seven days in a row. On the seventh day the walls of darkness around my heart were beginning to crumble too, just like the walls of Jericho.

At the end of the seventh day they moved me to another cell. I don't know if it was Satan trying to get me away from Rachel or God wanting me to take the next step. I believe now it was God.

When I had moved into my cell with Rachel I was given a top bunk. I began having seizures. My jailers worried about my falling out. So I was transferred to a cell with a bottom bunk.

If the devil wanted me away from Rachel he miscalculated. I did not expect to get a cellmate like Rachel. I fully expected to have a cellmate just like all the other cellmates I had ever had before: angry, defiant, acting just like me.

But God designed it otherwise! My new cellmate was Heather and she knew even more about the Bible than Rachel! She was a preacher's daughter! She had been brought up in Sunday school! How did she ever wind up here? She had fallen but no matter what kind of mess she was in at the moment, she still knew about the Bible, believed what it said and told me that the Bible had answers for my problems.

Whatever Rachel had done, Heather did more. She didn't just read Ephesians 6, she read other portions. She read stories to me that I knew almost nothing about. Heather became my Bible teacher. She read about Moses. She read about David, Daniel andthe Lion's Den, Jonah and the Whale, Job. She asked me about Samson and Delilah. I told her I had never heard of Samson and Delilah. She was surprised. Hadn't I ever seen Samson and Delilah on kid's cartoons? "Well, no." She read it. I was intrigued. I was intrigued by everything she did. I asked her to read the stories again and again.

My new friend on the unit, Missy Lee, got me a Bible. Wow—my very own Bible! I asked how I should read it since Heather would not be around forever and neither would Missy Lee. Missy Lee gave me advice. Start in the New Testament with John. Read about Jesus. I started marking the passages. That Bible would eventually be so marked up and worn it would begin to fall apart. It became my lifeblood.

As the days went by I began to want God. I did not just want help, like I had always prayed before. I wanted more. I wanted God. I wanted Jesus. There was a hunger in my heart. I knew about the craving for meth, but this was a new craving. This was a craving for God.

I am not sure how long it took, maybe a month and a half. I went to my new friend Missy Lee. God had put in my path the very kind of people who knew how to help me.

"Missy Lee, what do I need to do?

She opened the Bible. Romans 10:9:

If you confess with your mouth, "Jesus is Lord," and believe in your heart that God raised him from the dead, you will be saved. For it is with your heart that you believe and are justified, and it is with your mouth that you confess and are saved.

"Cynthia," she said, "you must get saved. You cannot get out of this mess yourself unless you are saved."

"How do I do that?"

Missy Lee knew these things. Whatever her problems—and she was in jail just like the rest of us—she knew about spiritual things.

"You have to believe. You believe that God loves you and he sent his son Jesus to die on the cross for your sins. You confess your sins and you believe God can save you. He will forgive your sins and make you one of his children."

I prayed just like Missy Lee told me. Chaplain Green helped me and led me in the sinner's prayer. All my life I longed for the love of a father, someone who could accept me in spite of everything I had done. God became that Father.

I prayed for God to forgive my sins. Heaven knows I had sins. There was nothing in me that would make me desirable to God. My whole life was a life of rebellion, doing things my way. Maybe I should try someone else's way—God's way.

God received me. It was not necessarily like a blinding light like what happened to Paul, but something definite happened to me. There was a hole in my heart that belonged to God and on that day He came to fill it. Paul would become my favorite Bible person. He spent time in jail just like me. He wrote my favorite passage in Ephesians, the one Rachel first read to me.

I wanted a new name. New creatures in Christ get new names, like Saul became Paul. Actually, all I wanted was the name I was supposed to have. I was named *Cynthia,* but all my life people called me *Cindy.* I didn't want to be Cindy anymore. People on the street called me Cindy. People in my old life called me Cindy. I believe God wanted me to be Cynthia. I asked my new friends to call me Cynthia and they did.

It is amazing as I think back on it. I was not saved the way most other Christians are saved. I was not saved in a Christian home. I did not grow up in Sunday school. I didn't know any of the children's songs or the Bible stories. I was not saved at a youth meeting. I was not saved at church camp or after a visit from church people who witnessed to me and taught me about Jesus. I was not saved from hearing a radio preacher. I was not saved in a church. To tell the truth I didn't know much at all about church. I didn't know much about Christians. I didn't know anything about Jesus. I didn't know that much about the Bible. I was not saved by some wise counselor who talked with me.

I was saved in jail. The people who helped me were people just like me. They were full of problems. They were in trouble. They had been arrested. Their lives were not straightened out. But God used them. Someone called them "wounded healers." They were wounded persons helping other wounded persons, sinners helping sinners, people with problems helping other people with problems.

Later when I discovered more of the Bible, I read these words:

> *Brothers, think of what you were when you were called. Not many of you were wise by human standards; not many were influential; not many were of noble birth. But God chose the foolish things of the world to shame the wise; God chose the weak things of the world to shame the strong. He chose the lowly things of this world and the despised things…so that no one may boast before him*
>
> —I Corinthians 1:26-28

It was my jail mates—weak and foolish and lowly, beaten down by the world—who helped me come to Christ.

I was happy. I am not sure I had ever been happy before in my whole life. I was not happy because of drugs; I was happy because of Jesus! I had been on the road to destruction and was just ready to step over the cliff. It amazes me that I did not die. Matt, the kids' dad, had died. Matt's dad, Tim, had died. Others I knew had died. I was in line, but God grabbed me just in time. I was alive. I met people who cared for me, even though they were jail mates. In the past, people who seemed to act nice to me were just wanting something from me. How different my new friends were! They sincerely wanted to help me.

I am thankful for jail. That must be hard for some people to believe. I am thankful for jail. I had food to eat and clothes to wear. I had joy in my heart. I had new friends. I had my Bible. What more could one ask for?

I sang. The best time was in the morning. We ate breakfast at 6:30, then it was time to pass meds (medicine) followed by room search. It all happened according to a schedule. Yet even that was a blessing. I had never been on a schedule, at least one I was willing to abide by. There was order in the routine. It was the same every day. I knew what to expect. And so I sang. I sang because I was happy:

Of course I didn't know any Christian songs. No choruses. No hymns. What I did know was Mr. Rogers TV song, so I sang that.

It's a beautiful day in the neighborhood.

Some of the women groaned. "Cynthia, how can you be so happy? We, after all, are in jail. Are you crazy? People don't sing in jail." But I sang. I sang because I was happy. I sang because I had food and people around me and my Bible. I began to learn Christian songs. I sang songs I heard Missy Lee sing. I made up songs.

The joy is mine, the joy is mine, the joy today is mine.

I started talking about my new love. I started talking about God. Not all of the girls were pleased. Some really resented any references to God. In their eyes I was obnoxious. People I knew before said I was fake. I had "jail religion." She'll get over it, they said. She'll get out of jail and go back to her old ways.

One of those who believed I would go back to the old ways was Robbie. This was not the first time I had gone to jail when I was hooked up with Robbie. Two other times it happened. Both other times when I got out of jail I was back with him. Robbie came to see me. In fact, he was the only one who came to see me from the outside. No family came. No one I might have considered friends came.

I told Robbie I was quitting. I told him I didn't want drugs any more. I told him I had found God. At first Robbie would not believe me. He too started talking about "jail religion." Lots of people in jail claimed to have found God but it didn't last. He thought I was the old Cindy Burch. He told me he could get drugs to me.

But I didn't give up. Jesus was in a lot of my talk and Robbie began to be uneasy. Then Robbie tried something different. One day he told me he was not using any more himself. He was done.

I knew he wasn't telling the truth. I had been around drugs too long. Even as he spoke to me he was high. He was jittery. He couldn't even talk straight. He cussed at me. We were in the jail, communicating by the phone through the thick glass. "Robbie, I cannot see you like this." I was referring to his being high on drugs. "You're not telling the truth."

I hung up the phone and walked off and left him. I am surprised at my boldness. I no longer belonged to Satan. I no longer belonged to Robbie. I belonged to God. The right thing to do was to walk away. Robbie was mad. He yelled, "Pick up the phone." I thank God for wisdom. I cared for Robbie, but I would not allow myself to be an enabler. I would not be nice just to avoid trouble.

Robbie then began to write letters to me. I wrote back. When I was ready to go to Richmond I wrote back and told him things were going to be different. He wasn't going to accept it. He tried to come and see me in Richmond. He borrowed a car or so he said. But I was not going to pretend we could build something on our old relationship. He came to Richmond. I could not hug him. In fact I didn't even want to be around him. It was too much a reminder of the old days. I told him I was no longer the person he thought he knew. Another time later he called and said he was on his way to see me. I had one of the nurses call back to tell him I had taken him off my visitor's list. I told him he couldn't see me. When one of the nurses called he told her he was lost. I don't know if he was truly lost or whether he was even on the way.

The next day the nurse called Robbie's number again. The cell phone was dead. I called his brother's house. His sister answered. The conversation had to be brief. We were allowed only four minutes on the phone. I got his sister's daughter. She gave me news.

"Did you hear what happened to Uncle Robbie? He blew the house up."

I shuddered. It was true. I could have been in that house. Robbie had bad burns on his arms, his hands, and his face.

A couple of days later someone told me to call Robbie again. It was December, 2008. I got him on the phone. He was on the run from the police. I begged him to turn himself in. He eventually did and is now in prison but I no longer have contact with him.

On his chest is a tattoo of my kids' names.

For July 4, 2008, less than three months after I was enslaved to meth, I wrote to the women on my unit. I wanted to encourage them:

Man has thrown us here. They have called us misfits. This is the place they throw people who they believe have no use in the world. But God sees otherwise. God has provided bed, clothes, blankets and food. Thank God! Not many people have these things.

I am not saying : "Praise God I'm in jail," because nobody wants to be here. I am saying what man thinks is wrong God says, 'This has a purpose.' God is pulling us to him. Tell me you don't believe that you are here in this group for prayer and faith. You are not here just to pass time, but because you want to know how to change your life. BIBLE. The answer to everything is in Him.

Today is Independence Day. I want you to see that you are free or can be completely free. Who could be more free than one who is free in the depths of her soul? Galatians 5:1 tells us that Christ has set us free. He wants us to enjoy freedom. So stand firm. Don't let the chains of slavery hold you again.

One day in those early weeks I found a small leaf in the rec area. It was a message from God. It was a sign. I was filled with the presence of God. I brought that leaf to my cell (actually I shouldn't have because we were not to bring anything from outside). I traced that leaf on a sheet of paper. I carry that leaf in my Bible today. It is as green as it was the day I found it. (Someone said it was because it was the Living Word). When I traced the leaf I wrote:

Dear God,

Your love is faithful and great. I have never been so happy! I can do nothing without you. I thank you for all you do in my life. I pray, Father, you will continue to help me grow and gain wisdom and strength. Father, I ask that you do your will in me and my life. I ask that you be with Ashley B's husband. Help him overcome the addiction. Take it out of his life. Help A.B, Father God, to grow in you. Thank you for my new bunkie N.W. Please help her with her sickness and do your will in her life. Please look after the people in this jail and all people. Thank you for my life and for everything you do and continue to do. Please help me to let go and let you. I'm having trouble with letting go. Please help me. And please look over and protect my kids T.A. F. Help me with that. I give it to you. Touch their hearts.

Please help Robbie with the addiction. Help him have an abundance of work to keep him busy and make money. I need you and only you. Please give a withdrawal from your bank. I am your child and I would like a financial withdrawal. Please be right by me. Guide me. Forgive me of my sins. Put a keeper on my tongue and lead my steps. I thank you. You are wonderful in all you do. I love you. You're awesome, the Almighty. You are the potter and I am the clay. Mold me.

Love, your daughter in Jesus' name. Amen.

That phrase "a keeper on my tongue" was a phrase I used a lot. I was still cursing. I had grown up cursing. It was a way of expressing my defiance. Maybe I thought I could control people with cursing.

It was Rachel that helped me. Rachel, the person God put in my path. "You don't have to curse. It does not glorify God."

"How can I stop?

It was Rachel who gave me the phrase. "Ask God to place a keeper on your tongue, so that words you speak may be worthy of Him. "

Slowly, over a period of months, God gave me control of my tongue.

I was healing in other ways, too: physically. Even in those first few weeks, the open sores began to heal. I didn't itch nearly as much. During the first several months in jail my cellmate Heather commented that the cell had a strange smell. "Don't you smell it, Cynthia?" she would say, "It smells like sulphur." Then one day I was washing my hair and I smelled it. I had been running my hands through my hair. They smelled like rotten eggs. The smell was from my body. My body was slowly purging the toxic waste of the meth.

But it was a good sign. The poison was draining from my body. I was gaining weight. The open sores were almost gone. I didn't need to scratch them any more.

Some time later I wrote about my jail experience:

I spent a lot of time in my cell but I made some friends whom I could share verses with and read with. When I first went in Missy Lee did the prayer group. She led it. I didn't talk a lot. I walked around looking at the floor. I was afraid of the people but I grew and grew closer to God. I started to find out what I needed to be filled with and that was the Holy Spirit. When Missy Lee left I led the prayer group. Who would have thought that the girl who never looked in the eyes of the other girls and who had trouble speaking would be able to speak for God and pray with the ladies when they came to me? I wanted to know God so I spent a lot of time in my cell looking in the Word and in prayer and in the Bible dictionary and the concordance. I did some fasting. Nothing big at first: bread, sweets, a meal. All my fasting has been for my relationship with God to grow. Then I spent six and a half months with no meat.

I met my attorney, Matt, in jail. I knew him. He had been my attorney many times before. He told me I needed drug court. I believed I needed in-patient treatment.

I believe it was the conviction that I had to have the right people in my life that led me to insist that I needed more than just the Drug Court Program. In that program I would live someplace outside of jail but would attend sessions and counseling authorized by the courts. But where could I stay? I had been banned from the one place that might have had me and that was Open Arms, the women's shelter of the Kokomo Rescue Mission.

I was afraid to leave jail, if that is possible. I had just started to get my head screwed on straight. I realized I didn't know how to deal with life apart from drugs. I was beginning to be realistic about how weak and vulnerable I was. I had always thought I could handle things myself. Now I knew I couldn't. I had never lived in a world apart from the drug scene. I wouldn't even know how to act. I spoke to Reba Harris of Gilead House. She was one of the many people that helped me. She did classes in jail. She said to talk to someone about it. Talk to the drug court people. Maybe I needed an in-residence program. I talked to my probation officer, Laura Rood. She agreed; some people need more than the court program.

The time was approaching for me to leave jail. I needed an assessment. The assessment was done by Linda Gilbert. Linda worked at St. Joe hospital with IOP (Intensive Outpatient Treatment). There are a lot of people that work with the courts, people in social work and people who do counseling. But they weren't the people I needed. I didn't know how to talk to them. When I met Linda Gilbert it was different. I felt she cared. I felt free to talk to her and so when she asked if there were anything else I might need to tell her I spoke of my fear of going back into the community. I needed in-residence help. Linda would be my counselor in IOP, the program I needed to be in, but she was sensitive to the fact that she alone might not be able to help me to live clean in the world. She would be an advocate.

A few days later I got the word: I would go to Richmond State Hospital. I didn't even know there was a Richmond State Hospital! But I was willing. Not just willing. I was eager. I had been in the Howard County Correctional Facility for six months. I look now at those six months as one of the most important times in my life. I entered a broken drug addict; I left a child of God. I entered so crushed that I could hardly speak to people. I left as a person who could lead a prayer group. Jail was like my spiritual retreat. I thank God for the jail.

Before I left jail I wrote a poem:

I used to claim my addictions, my burdens and my pains,
I used to claim I was better, and had everything to gain.
I used to claim it was fine to be high and out of my mind.
I used to claim I was a good mother all the time.
I used to claim it was OK to lie, steal, cheat, and break the law;
I used to claim I'd stay the same, I'd never change, I would always make, sell, and shoot up drugs.
I used to claim that I was loved,
But I lied, until one night I cried.
Please dear God, take it all away.
I pray this in Jesus' name.
That was the day I went to jail.
That was the day I was freed from my own personal hell;
So hear me when I say,
Those are the things I used to claim.

Now I claim a new life, and a chance to live right,
With God at my side!
So hear me when I say, those are the things I used to claim;
So hear me when I say, those are the things I used to claim;
SO HEAR ME WHEN I SAY, THOSE ARE THE THINGS I USED TO CLAIM!

I said good-bye to my friends at the jail and prepared for Richmond. I was ready for a new chapter in my life.

CHAPTER 13

Richmond

I went to Richmond State Hospital on November 5, 2008. This was uncharted territory for me—all new. I knew jail. I knew the streets. I didn't know what to expect at a state hospital. One thing I did know. I needed more help and this promised more help. I was ready but nervous. I prayed that God would go before me and place all the right people in my life. It was a two-hour drive in a paddy wagon—cuffed and shackled. The only things I had were the clothes on my back, my Bible, a few hygiene products—and a renewed spirit. The important part was the renewed spirit. God was with me. I spent the two-hour trip wondering what it would be like. Would it help me? I prayed. I also thought about the friends I had made in jail that I was leaving behind.

When I arrived I was searched, went through a physical check-up, and was fed. I remember the dessert was strawberry and banana mix with whipped cream. I was so grateful.

There were a lot of new people who welcomed me but I did not know how to be around them. I was aware of how socially inadequate I was. At this point in my life I had no friends except for the friends I had made in jail. But I could not have contact with them. The only person I knew who might ever visit me was Robbie. On three different occasions when I was with Robbie and I was in jail he came to see me. He would probably have come to Richmond but I didn't want to see him. He now was part of an old life I wanted to leave behind. My mom would not come, nor my sisters, nor any of my aunts and uncles. So I felt alone in the world.

I realized later that, except for jail, I had not had to relate to a lot of people since I was clean. That is, relate in a normal way, the way other people relate. This was true especially of men. I didn't know what to say to guys. It was strange. When I was stripping men were around all the time. But it was another world, an unreal world. I had to have drugs just to be able to talk to those men. But now I was in a different world. The only men I had known up to this time other than my drug friends or guys in the strip clubs were police or chaplains. So when I went to Richmond if one of the guys sat next to me I would jump up and move away.

But God is good. I don't think it is my natural personality to be afraid of people. Soon I was talking. I was making friends. I loved the staff. They soon became my family.

One day an amazing thing happened which I had not expected. I had meth rot of my teeth. I was in constant pain just trying to eat regular food. The hospital staff was able to get dental work for me. My old teeth were pulled and I received dentures. I could smile.

We did a lot of group things at Richmond. We did counseling. I loved it! Can people actually love being at a state hospital? Well, I did.

Thanksgiving, 2008

I woke up this morning thinking, "Wow! Thank God, I'm alive. This time last year—I can only say I was so high I can't ever recall recognizing it was Thanksgiving—laid up with a needle in my arm. If I could only explain how much it means to me to be clean. This time last year I claimed I'd never change. I was a hopeless wreck.

Richmond is a state hospital. It is not necessarily a Christian place. Yet I found some Christian friends. We started a Bible study. I was able to go to church.

On Christmas day, 2008, I wrote to my kids:

I went to the Christmas party even though I didn't want to at first. I found that I enjoyed it. There was a child there about ten. We watched the Suite Life of Zack and Cody. It helped me even though you were not with me.

I realized again God loves me and there is so much to enjoy in life. There is so much more to enjoy than I can imagine—like a moment to giggle at a TV show with a child, like talking with friends who care, like the home setting with the footprints picture on the wall and the blue blotch of paint with the border at the ceiling.

It is great to see life as it is meant to be, to see things clean and people having fun. I remember seeing things today that mean so much. When I was using these things meant nothing. Things like how pretty it is outside, like the warm feeling I felt inside when God filled me up.

I have a job in the kitchen. It's cool. I am working with girls I like. Especially Elaine. She is cool—I mean nice. I love her. I've been noticing small things that never seemed important before, like the way my crosses jingle. I worked last night. It was so beautiful.

Love, Mom

Of course not all the days were good.

January 12, 2009

Dear God,

I need you to be with me. It is so hard here. People are not very nice. I know you can do anything and I believe that I've seen you move mountains. You know all I've been through. Father, please allow your will in my life. Lead and guide me. Protect me. Keep me safe. Double your armor up on me. Please forgive me of my sins. Please be with my kids. I miss them. Protect them. Be with Jeff. Help him to be OK and get better. Lead him. Be with Robbie. Be with the girls in jail and everyone here and all people. God, please protect me. I love you so much. In Jesus' name, Amen.

But on the next day I wrote.

January 13, 2009

Nine months clean. Thank God. This is the greatest accomplishment in my life. It is so hard but I want it so bad. I am powerless over my addiction. If I pick it up again I will die. I want this more than I ever wanted anything in my life. It's not going to be easy and at times I feel like giving up. I need to remember all I've made it through thus far. I am so happy I've met all the RSH staff. They are so helpful and they are there for me. I've made it nine months. I have the rest of my life to go.

February 10, 2009

Jason left today. We all told him good-bye. I will miss him around here. It seems when some people leave we never talk about them again. They fade away. But others remain in our hearts forever because they made an impact and we remember that. I just want to learn what I need to take with me to live a clean and sober life. I want to learn how to stay sober. I am grateful to be here. I am grateful for Sandy, Carolyn, Tim, and staff, for my peers, for the outside, for the birds and the clouds and my bed and the room and for clothes to wear, for my job, for sobriety, for the reflection the CD gives, and for life itself.

March 10, 2009

I completed all my work today. I have completed the program. I am happy about that but I think a lot about Angel, Trent, and Faith. I know God is with them and looking over them. I just miss and love them.

This was supposed to be a ninety-day program. At the end of ninety days they knew and I knew I still needed to be there. Could I stay for another ninety days? I got a hold of Matt Elkin, my attorney, and asked if he could get the court date postponed. He did. It was approved. I could stay.

March 15, 2009

I have been lazy today. I've slept most of the day. I went to work at 4:45 and took out trash at one point in time today and realized I slept through a beautiful day and was a little upset with myself over it. I want to do things right and wonder if there is a way to be or act and if there is something wrong with me. I'm trying to see that I am changing but I don't see much change where I need a change. I think a lot is inside but do I? I am confused. I just pray to make it through another day.

I am grateful for God (#1). To be sober another day (#2). My kids to see TJ (3#). My friends, peers, Todd who helps me everyday (#4). I am grateful to be happy with my staff (#5).

March 23, 2009

Today is Matt's b-day. I'm sober. Seven years ago he died of an overdose. It is so hard for me to handle losing him. I thought I'd be OK. I remember after he died having a birthday party and cake. It was like a final birthday. I was so zoned out, me and Ang dropped the cake. But still laughed and ate it. Dana left. That's what made me a mess as soon as he walked out the door. I remembered the time the cops came and took the kids. I sent the care bears with them and said that those bears would love them for me. I promised it would be all right. I have problems with that—with promising and not being there now, but I did it myself. I am grateful for them; I am sober and alive. I know I am a good person who is loveable, loving, and kind. I am a sweet and kind-hearted person. The sun is pretty. The dance was fun. I am spoiled and learning a lot of people love me.

On another occasion:

I keep getting this picture in my mind. It starts with Matt in his casket. Trent is crying, saying how bad he will miss his number one daddy. I see Matt's body so cold and hard. I knew then we would never be back together again. My heart hurts. Then my mind goes to the time the police came to my place with guns pulled at me and my kids.

Even though my sins are forgiven through Jesus Christ, and even though God has set my feet in a different direction, a direction so that my life will be pleasing to Him, and I can serve him, the ugly past is always there. Maybe God puts it in my mind

Then there was a horrible set-back. The word came that a decision had been made about my kids: Trent, April, and Crystal Faith. It was always my hope and dream that once I had finished the program at Richmond and once I had proved that I had left the old life, that I could be reunited with my family.

It evidently was not to be. The word was sent: I was to lose custody. Not only that, I would not be allowed to see my kids nor contact them. They were to break ties with me and start life afresh with someone else. I was crushed. I was screaming. I was mad. Mad at God. Was all of this rehabilitation for nothing? Did they not take into account I was clean? I had started on a new path. My life was turned around. Didn't that matter at all? Oh God, why is this happening to me? I flipped out.

It is probably a good thing I was in Richmond when this word came. Who knows what would have happened to me if I had been on my own. I was in danger of losing everything I had worked for.

God had to teach me a lesson. Jesus was to be my life, with my kids or without them. My life was to be lived for Him. He would have something in store for me. If everything were easy we would not have to live by faith.

The second ninty days passed. It was time for me to leave. I gained so much from Richmond State Hospital. I saw things in a different way. It was the beginning of my new life. I hoped I might stay in Richmond. I didn't want to return to Kokomo. I could not see my kids. I had no friends there except the girls in jail. The people who knew me knew me as Cindy the addict. I was not that person any more. I did not want to be associated with that person. I did not even want to be in contact with people who thought of me that way. I was afraid of relapse. I guess I did not trust myself. There were several places I could go to in Richmond. Half-way houses. I had spent time at Victory House, a Christian-based ministry. That's where I wanted to go.

My attorney, Matt, the public defender, would have none of it. I belonged in Kokomo. They would never give me permission not to come back. If I didn't come, he would make sure a warrant was issued for my arrest. I was told I needed to be in the Drug Court Program.

On May 4 (my daughter's eighth birthday), 2009, I was cuffed once again and came back to Kokomo the same way I had left: the same paddy wagon, the same driver, probably the same cuffs.

I was scared. I had been clean only for just a little over a year. The only thing I knew waiting for me in Kokomo was my old life. I felt vulnerable. I felt alone. I felt I wasn't capable of being on my own. I really needed God's presence. I needed the Holy Spirit. I prayed once again that God would put the right people in my life. I would put myself in God's hands. What did he have for me?

I should not have been scared. Don't the Scriptures say:

Eye hath not seen, nor ear heard, nor the heart of man conceived, what God has prepared for those who love him.

—I Cor. 2:9

Cynthia Burch

CHAPTER 14

Open Arms

Cynthia Burch and Kem Howell at Open Arms

When I came back to Kokomo from Richmond in May of 2009, I was put in jail. Believe it or not, that was okay with me. I felt vulnerable again. I didn't have any place to go. If they had turned me loose I am sure that within an hour I would have found Robbie, or if not him, someone else from my old life. Jail was a safe place. I was there for two months.

I prayed that God would put the right people in my life. I knew the right people would be the Kokomo Rescue Mission and Open Arms but I had been banned from there. The words that had been spoken against me in court when I lost custody of my kids were stuck in my mind: *"Persons like her never change."* Those words hurt. People, even good people, did not really trust me. They may have heard that my life was different, but of course many addicts have used that argument. Addicts say anything to get out of trouble.

Maybe I wasn't 100% sure myself that God had broken the bondage for good. That's why I preferred jail rather than to risk any kind of exposure to my old life.

I grew up only a few blocks from the mission but had not known much about it. There would have been food there, and clothes. But my parents either did not know about, or they wanted to avoid, the mission. The mission, after all, had rules. They would have pushed religion. The mission would be against the kind of life we were leading.

When I found out about the Kokomo Rescue Mission later in life I discovered that it was place of help. One time—I remember the year, 1998—I needed deposit money for an apartment. Bob Cox, director of the mission, gave it to me. He also prayed with me.

When I was on the streets with my kids we ate at the mission regularly. We would walk across town for a meal. We did this often over the period of a year. The meals were free and they didn't ask embarrassing questions. My kids hated the walk; sometimes it was cold, sometimes it was in the rain. But there was no place else to eat. I was getting food stamps at the time, but I had sunk so low that I was either selling the stamps (which is illegal) or trading for drugs. The mission would feed us. The mission also gave us clothes.

I then heard that the mission had started a program for women and children. I checked them out three times when they were still in the yellow house on Taylor Street, in September of 1999, in December of 1999, and in July of 2000. In each instance, I filled out an application but I didn't stay, even one night. The rules turned me off. I wanted to be free, though I had a false view of freedom. My idea of freedom was doing what I wanted to do when I wanted to do it. Instead of freedom it was really bondage because "what I wanted to do" was controlled by *"the cravings of the sinful nature"* (Eph. 2:3). I was a slave to principalities and powers.

I tried Open Arms again several years later, in July of 2005, when the shelter had moved to Main Street (where it is now), but again I did not stay overnight. Maybe I wasn't desperate enough.

By May of 2006 I was desperate. My kids were with me and I wasn't able to care for them. I told Open Arms I would live by the rules, but of course I was lying. While I was there I remember they took me to church at First General Baptist. I remember they wanted me to take a drug class but I couldn't because I had failed the drug test. I failed a lot of things. I was violating the rules of Open Arms. I would send my kids to school and then leave and see Robbie. I would sneak out during the day to go to other places. My attitude was bad. Ms. Kem was teaching a parenting class and I was angry, thinking that I knew better than she or anyone else how I should raise my kids. I must have stayed a couple of weeks. When Ms. Kem found out about what was going on she said I would have to leave.

Now where would I go?

I called a woman I knew in a class that Open Arms had forced me to take and she got me in touch with Jeff McKay, a police officer that had been involved with my kids at the school. He put me up in a motel room and called Child Protection Services (CPS). CPS then called Open Arms and asked them to give me another chance.

Another chance? There was no possibility that would work. I didn't want to go back to Open Arms but I had no other choice. No one else was going to be putting me up in a motel. So I went back. I stayed at Open Arms that time for about a week. Again I did not follow rules. I did not listen. Finally when the first of the month came I got the social security check I was receiving for my kids. I now had some money so I didn't need Open Arms. I was ready to clear out.

I did not leave graciously. I vented all my anger and frustration on the way out. The scene in the parking lot was not pretty.

My kids were with me. Miss Krista and Miss Brenda were there. I had been confronted about some of the things I had been doing. I went into a screaming tirade. I yelled about how Open Arms never helped anyone. I told them they were all hypocrites and liars. They told me if I left I could never come back. I left. So I was banned. I was too disruptive. I was not good for the morale of the place.

That is why, when I came back from Richmond Open Arms did not seem like an option for me. Did Open Arms also believe what had been spoken in my presence?

Persons like her never change.

I was beginning to wonder. That's why I was stuck in jail. I had completed the program (twice) at Richmond. I needed to be in the Drug Court Program in Kokomo, but I could not enter the program without a place to stay.

God intervened.

Persons like her never change.

The world may have thought that I could never change, but God knew better. God and Open Arms and the Kokomo Rescue Mission are in the business of changing lives.

Ms. Krista had read the report from Richmond. I'm pretty sure it didn't say anything about Jesus, but it said I had made good progress and was trying to live clean. Of course all the addicts say they are trying to live clean, so that didn't mean much.

But Open Arms is called Open Arms for a reason. They sent word that I could come back.

To rescue is their mission,
to care as they share,
They have arms open wide.

Never a place to call home…
never a place to feel safe…
never to feel peace or feel free
Until God brought all of these things to me,
Men and women who ask nothing in return,
The gift they give warms my heart and fills me with love inside

To rescue is their mission,
to care as they share
They have arms open wide

Open arms is what you'll see,
Open arms is what they have given me,

A fresh new start,
Peace and love in my heart.

—Cynthia Burch, 10-17-09

I remember that it was just before July 4, 2009. I was back in court. My attorney, Matt Elkin, was with me. Judge Menges assigned me to Open Arms and also to the Drug Court Program, a rehabilitation program for drug offenders. I would have to report five times a week, take drug tests three times a week, attend AA or NA (Narcotics Anonymous) meetings, go to group counseling, and go to court once a week. I could start immediately but because of the holiday I would have to spend two more days in jail. Then I could go to Open Arms.

When court was dismissed I got up to leave and return to jail but my attorney Matt Elkin told me to sit down. I didn't understand and said, "Court is over." He said, "No, sit down." So I sat down. Then an amazing thing happened. Judge Menges came down from his bench and pulled up a chair, and started talking with me. Court was over. He could leave. Usually with court it is all business: get in and get out. But this was different: a personal conversation. I was certainly no stranger to him. I had been before him—I can't even remember the times—maybe on fifteen different occasions. Four different times he had sent me to jail. He personified authority and all my life I hated authority. When you talked to the judge you said, "Yes, sir," and "No, sir." We were hardly friends. I was a common criminal. I was cuffed and in shackles. I was not anyone.

The judge didn't threaten or condemn me. He didn't treat me like a criminal. He was encouraging. I don't remember much of what he said. I think I was too overwhelmed. The judge talking to me? I was encouraged. God was putting the right people in my life.

I wondered how they would receive me at Open Arms, especially after the trouble I had caused. I went there directly from jail. I went as a new person, not as the person they had known—Cindy Burch—but the redeemed person, Cynthia Burch. When I walked through the door, Ms. Kem, the director, shook her head. She remembered Cindy Burch, the dirty, unkempt, angry, sullen and cursing woman. She hardly recognized the new person, Cynthia Burch, smiling, happy, and with Jesus on her face. She wasn't sure it was me. "You're so different. Is this the same Cynthia Burch?" Well, it wasn't the same Cynthia Burch. Not the old Cindy Burch she knew. This was the new Cynthia Burch. I was smiling. I was happy. What was the difference? Jesus. Jesus was in my life and on my face. Ms. Kem gave me a big hug.

I was so thankful to be there. The first day I just touched the grass and enjoyed the outdoors. It was my first day of freedom. I wrote a letter to my kids. Someday maybe I can share it personally with them.

July 8, 2009

For Trent, Angel and Faith:

I spent my first night here staring out the window at the most beautiful full moon I have ever seen in my whole life. Thanks God!

I went to IOP (Intensive Outpatient Program) yesterday and I enjoyed it! I really feel that this program has been given by God, every part of it, even staying at Open Arms. I am so blessed. I enjoy looking at the birds and hearing them sing. The sun is warm. The grass is green. I am so grateful to be out of jail and sober. It is great. It is God.

Trent, Angel and Faith: I miss you so much. I think about you every day and I know someday I will see you again. Oh, I've thought about how big you have grown. I think of your smiles. I know God is with you. I bet you're enjoying your summer. I bet you are swimming. I miss swimming with you. You all could swim when you were still in diapers. You were born swimmers. I bet you have many talents (like your Mom).

I am finding God has given me talents and gifts that I never knew about or thought about.

Well, my beautiful babies. I love you with a love that never ends.

Love forever and always,
Mommy

One of the first things that happened to me at Open Arms was that I was given a schedule detailing when to get up in the morning and what was expected of me—to clean my area, to prepare for breakfast, to get to breakfast on time. That certainly would not be different for anyone else, but it was for me. A routine was something I should have learned as a kid, but I never did. When I was growing up I was on my own. There were no expectations. No one checked up on me. No one cared enough to hold me accountable. Now there were expectations. I had to report to drug court. If I didn't there were consequences. It is terrible to say, but they were teaching me to grow up and it was like I had to start at the beginning.

To help we got a paper, called Self-Evaluation. It was not meant to be a judgment. It was a way of stopping for a moment and seeing whether what we were doing was right or wrong. It was helping us to be better persons. I was learning how to be a woman.

Open Arms was soon like home. It was family. I never had a family. I never had a place where I felt I belonged, where someone cared about what was happening to me, where someone could laugh with me when I laughed, or cry with me when I cried. When I was out and told someone I had to go home, home was Open Arms.

Open Arms was like a school. I took Dave Boss's class on Christian studies; I took a class on finances. I had a class on boundaries. I had one on goal setting; one was called the Almond Tree class and one was called Changes That Heal. I took all the classes I could get. I went to all the Bible studies.

Open Arms was like a community of believers. Not everyone there was a believer (we had a Muslim once); many had not yet come to know Jesus. But the prevailing spirit was one of a group where Christ was at the center, where we could pray, and talk about spiritual things.

Open Arms is not what people might expect when they think of a women's shelter run by a rescue mission. It is not a big room with beds lined up in a run-down building. Open Arms is a place where women and children can go when they are homeless. It is a safe place. You can be yourself. There is a lounge, a kitchen to use, a play area for children, and nice rooms where two could stay, or even four, or six. A mother could be with her children. The rooms are decorated with nice wall paper and named after women of the Bible: Ruth, Deborah, Hannah. The beds are named after the precious stones in the Bible: rubies, diamonds, emeralds, amethysts.

The staff members didn't act like wardens in an institution. They mingled. Persons who came in from the outside might not even know who were the staff and who were the residents. Ms Kem, the director, was in charge. She had authority over me, yet often I would think of her as a sister, or a friend, or a mentor or counselor.

The people who came to Open Arms were sometimes people in need of a place to stay for a night or several nights. But many of them were also hurting; they were the spiritually broken. They were people with problems. At Open Arms they came into contact with people who cared. More importantly the people who cared, staff or volunteers, were people who knew Jesus and were willing to share how Jesus can change lives.

I really felt comfortable at Open Arms. They and the drug court were helping me deal with my past. I had many chances to witness. I would talk to the ladies about Jesus, about my life, and about deliverance from an ugly past. I was soon given more responsibilities. After a while I became a paid intern. I was in charge when the other staff members were not there. I had my own private quarters. I had a door to the outside.

On October 27, 2009, I graduated from the program at Open Arms. I gave my testimony and received a diploma. It was one of the happiest days of my life.

CHAPTER 15

The Setback and the Armor of God

Therefore put on the full armor of God, so that when the day of evil comes, you may be able to stand your ground, and after you have done everything, to stand. —Ephesians 6:13

I really liked Open Arms. I was learning so much. I was growing spiritually. My life finally seemed to be straightened out. Still—I think of this now though I did not think of it then—I was a relatively new Christian. Despite the joy of Jesus in my heart, I was still not fully covered with the armor of God. Despite all of the battles that I had fought—or rather that Jesus had fought on my behalf—with the powers of evil, in certain areas of my life I was still weak and vulnerable to powers of the spirit world. There was (and is) so much I needed to learn.

I am convinced Christian believers can never rest assured that once defeated, Satan will not attack again.

Be self-controlled and alert. Your enemy the devil prowls around like a roaring lion looking for someone to devour.
—I Peter 5:8

It happened to me. Satan sought to devour my soul. What happened to me nearly destroyed me, my victory in Christ, my new life, and the joy that meant so much to me.

I had always thought that if I were to sin and fall, it would be because I saw someone from my old life, or because the powerful attraction of drugs would overpower me in a weak moment.

That is not the way it was. After I had been at Open Arms about five months and things seemed to be going well, I stumbled. Someone has said that when Satan tempts you he never comes as an ugly devil with a pitchfork, but as a friend. An ugly devil we can resist; it is much harder to resist evil disguised as someone we trust.

I wanted friends. I loved everyone but I wanted a close friend, someone I could confide in. A woman named Annie (not her real name) took an interest in me. She paid a lot of attention to me. We began to do things together. I could talk to her. Some persons felt uneasy about our relationship—I was spending way too much time with her—but I was convincing myself there was nothing inappropriate about our friendship. She made me feel good. I could speak to her about Jesus. I wanted her to know the joy I felt.

But this wasn't developing as a healthy relationship. I became emotionally attached to her, and then physically involved. I crossed lines I should not have crossed. All of the sudden I was in another form of addiction. I was being consumed by another person. I was confused about my sexuality.

I knew it was wrong. I had a guilty conscience. A guilty conscience? In a sense this was a new experience. I grew up without a conscience. No one talked to me about right and wrong. I didn't ever think in terms of right and wrong. When my dad beat me I never believed I had done anything wrong. I was never punished because I really deserved it, at least in my eyes. My dad just beat me because that was his nature; he got satisfaction from hurting people, even his own family. It was the same with my sisters and in the fights we had. If they did something I didn't like we would fight. Our parents never told us it was wrong. I never had the sense I shouldn't be doing this. In fact my dad would urge us on. It was survival of the fittest. I once clamped a hot curling iron around my sister Loretta's leg and squeezed it until her flesh was smoking (she still has a scar). She screamed and screamed. I wouldn't let up. I never felt any remorse for that.

And it got a lot worse than curling irons. I took drugs. I sold drugs. I saw people that I sold drugs to get messed up. I sold drugs to underage kids and, I am sure, led some into addiction. I cursed. I stole. I lied. I was a stripper. I manipulated. I slept around. At one time I was involved with persons who talked not only of getting even or beating up someone for money owed, but even of killing. I could have been involved in crimes that would have sent me to jail for years (by God's grace it never happened). In none of that did I feel remorse. Or maybe remorse was there but I didn't acknowledge it. I know now that all these things made me feel miserable. But I never analyzed the cause of my misery. I never understood it as guilt. Instead of dealing with the pain and what caused it I would dull it with drugs.

But now that I had accepted Christ, I couldn't go to drugs. I had to live in the real world. The Holy Spirit had put this sense of right ands wrong in me and it was making me miserable. Sometimes something that feels good isn't right and it isn't glorifying to God. I was experiencing guilt. I was experiencing shame. It must have been like Eve in the garden the first time she sinned. She wanted to cover up. I wanted to cover up like Eve; I wanted to hide, hide from God and from the people I knew. It was poisoning my relationship with others. I was getting critical and finding fault with things at Open Arms. I was trapped in another kind of bondage. I would go home after hanging out with Annie and pray that God would get me out of this. But I didn't know how.

It was the old Cindy Burch coming back. I was rationalizing my behavior. I fell in with a group of Annie's friends who told me that what I was doing was perfectly all right. God made me that way. Everything I was doing was perfectly normal and approved by God. I knew otherwise, and even though I was praying to God I was thinking maybe I could handle this by myself. I couldn't. I knew I should tell someone, but I couldn't. I didn't know how. It was like when I was a little girl and was being beaten but I couldn't admit it was so.

But God had put a right person in my life. Ms. Kem had spiritual discernment. She knew all was not well with me. She asked me several times. "Cynthia, are you all right?" Of course I said everything was fine. Nothing was the matter. I lied. And that made me feel even more miserable. She did know about my relationship with Annie but she did not know everything.

One night she found out I had been sneaking out. She confronted me. There was no hiding it any more. There was a horrible scene. My sins were exposed to the light. I sobbed and sobbed.

Ms. Kem said, "What is it, Cynthia, you can tell me."

So I told her what was going on. Confession. The horrible truth. To speak it was so painful. When it was over there was a sense of relief—I no longer had to hide it—but now I had to face consequences. Now I was in trouble. I had broken the rules of Open Arms. It was more serious because I was an intern with special responsibilities. I had violated the trust put in me. I had broken the rules of drug court (no relationships with anyone else in the drug program). I was witnessing to one life but living another. Worst of all, I had sinned against God. I could never face the women at Open Arms again. It would soon be all over. I remember calling Hillarie, Matt's wife. "I'm in a relationship and this will cause my downfall." She had cared so much about me. I wanted her to hear it from me and not from anyone else.

Persons like her never change. Was it true?

Hillarie came to see me. I had to confess it again. I had to live the pain again.

I was now facing the downfall I had spoken to Hillarie about. I was relieved of my intern's job at Open Arms. I was in danger of being kicked out of drug court. The Drug Court Program was my lifeline. A 20-year jail sentence was a real possibility. I felt like a failure. I felt like a discarded rag.

I spoke with my probation office, Laura Rood. I had violated the terms of my probation. She would make a recommendation as to what would happen to me. I told her, "Just put me back in jail." At least I would be safe in jail. I wouldn't have to face people. I still loved God. I would love God in jail. I was safe there. I had been there before. It seemed the easy way out. I could be like a cloistered nun.

But God was putting right people in my life. Neither God nor others were giving up on me.

"Our struggle is not against flesh and blood..."

Some people were coming alongside of me and helping me in the struggle. God was assembling a spiritual army.

Laura spoke to me directly: "You have to work through this, Cynthia. Jail is not the answer."

But I wanted jail. Is it possible that persons who could be free would prefer jail?

Laura said, "Are you saying you would be willing to spend 20 years in jail?"

I went to jail for three days. It was a miserable three days. Was it three days in the belly of the big fish like Jonah? Was God preparing me so I could be spit out to do His work?

My attorney Matt Elkin came to see me in jail. I believe he came to battle against principalities and powers. He was another right person at the right time. He must have been sent by the drug court, or the judge, or God. Matt is the public defender. He had known me since I was 19. He had seen me at my worst. Even in the worst of those times he had tried to reach out to me. Originally, when I first knew him, his office was in his house. When I went there I had this feeling that I was not in a house but a home. I had never ever really been in someone's *home,* that is, where there were families that loved each other. The houses I had been in were partying houses or drug houses. The first times I went to Matt's I was defiant. He would talk to me and I would think: "Cut out the talk. Just get me off. Do your job and get me out of this, whatever the charges are."

Later at Open Arms Matt and his wife Hillarie opened their home to me. They invited me to Bible studies. Hillarie was pastoring a church, Never Too Young Ministries, and I attended there. They picked me up and took me into their home. I was amazed at the way she mothered her children. It was by the Bible. I helped Hillarie clean one of her rental properties. One day I helped make blackberry jam. Matt and Hillarie had gone the second mile, and the third, and the fourth. It occurred to me one day that while I called everyone else in authority with terms of respect, like *Judge* Menges, and *Ms.* Kem, and the policemen *officers,* somehow or other I had started calling Mr. Matthew Elkin *Matt,* like a friend.

So Matt came to the jail. Was I expecting condemnation? If so that is not what I got. It was not like he was a public defender trying to work out the best sentence for me. It was more like he was a father talking to a daughter.

"Don't give up, Cynthia. You can't always run away from troubles. Cynthia, all your life you have been running. You ran to drugs when the pain was heavy. You didn't want to face your problems. You need to fight, Cynthia. You need to fight for something good, something right."

Then it was more than just like a father. It was like he was an angel, like God speaking. Not an angel like a cherub, a baby angel that is cute; not a comforting angel that wipes your brow. This was a warrior angel with a flaming sword. He was a public defender; that was his training. But on this occasion he was not defending in the public court. He was defending against the charges of Satan. Satan wanted the soul of Cythnia Burch, and he was not going to let it happen.

"Don't be stupid, Cynthia. Don't let this happen. You didn't come this far to be defeated." These were not kind, understanding words. These were strong, harsh, straightforward words. He was rebuking demons. Some of what he said shouldn't even be repeated.

> *Therefore put on the full armor of God, so that when the day of evil comes, you may be able to stand your ground, and after you have done everything, to stand. Stand firm then, with the belt of truth buckled around your waist, with the breastplate of righteousness in place, and with your feet fitted with the readiness that comes from the gospel of peace. In addition to all this, take up the shield of faith, with which you can extinguish all the flaming arrows of the evil one.*
>
> —Eph. 6:13-16

I turned. At that moment I turned. I would fight. Running could not be the answer. How do these people know me so well?

I said, "OK, Matt."

I came out of jail on a Monday. Over the weekend people had been talking, people involved in my life. These were conversations I knew nothing about. These were people connected with the drug court, and with Open Arms. They were my counselors, the judge, the public defender, the Kokomo Rescue Mission, Open Arms. What should happen to Cynthia? Once I believed no one cared for me. I was a nobody. But I believe now that God had put together a mighty army and they were going to battle on my behalf.

They could have kicked me out of drug court. They could have kicked me out of Open Arms. By strict law I should have stayed in jail. Their decision: I should go back to Open Arms.

My problems were by no means over. For one, Annie was still around. She had left Open Arms and had been living at home. Because she had violated probation she was put in jail. But that did not deter her. She would not let go. She was determined that whatever the consequences, our relationship should continue. She started sending me notes. She would give letters to women at Open Arms and they would give them to me. The letters tore me up. I responded to some of the letters. That was a mistake. I wanted her to stop but it was hard to be forceful. The letters threatened; they pleaded; some were angry. Annie blamed me. She was in jail and I was not. I was at Open Arms and she was not. She told me it was my fault as much as hers. When people left jail they contacted me and told me Annie still loved me. Once a woman came to Open Arms and hugged me and told me that was for Annie. One day Annie wrote a letter quoting Scripture. It was a misuse of the Bible. I knew then that it was an evil design.

Secondly, I was still dealing with a terrible sense of guilt. When I was saved in jail, I was not experiencing guilt. I was experiencing bondage. I was under a curse, but other people had laid the curse on me. God broke the curse.

This time I faced guilt. It was not what someone else had done to me. It was what I had done to myself. I was at Open Arms, where I had always felt love and acceptance, but now it was different. I had violated trust. I had sinned. I was not sure how the other women felt about me. Worse, I was not sure how God felt about me. I had pleaded for forgiveness but the joy was not there. Shame accompanies guilt, and I felt shame. I didn't want to talk with people. I wore a sweatshirt with a hood that I would pull down to cover part of my face.

But I was not abandoned. God was dealing with me. If there was anything good that came from what I call *My Setback* it was from the realization that I needed to go deeper in confronting my past. Part of breaking the bondage of darkness was to let God's power cleanse everything in me, everything that I have done or that has happened to me. Someone told me I was passing from childhood to adulthood. I was learning not to run or hide from my problems, and not to cover them over with drugs, or with excuses. I was learning not to give in and take the easy way out. I had to face problems myself. I had to take responsibility before God.

It has not been pretty. It is one thing to be saved and forgiven. It is another thing to be cleansed and healed from the ugliness within. Healing takes place with honesty, and honesty hurts. How many times have I cried when I begin to see myself as I really was? I sometimes think if I had to mention the ugliest person I ever knew it would be me. I often saw, and still today see, the years of my life in flashbacks. I see myself standing and yelling at my kids because they wanted me but I was not wanting them. I would say I wanted them but I really wanted dope.

I didn't see or understand at the time what I was doing to others and to myself. I was so sick. The drug was all I wanted. It was my life, my love. I don't know if I could even add up the total cost of what I spent on drugs. But the dollar amount is not the worst. The cost of my addiction is the loss of my children. What every mother wants: to touch and hold and kiss her kids and tell them she loves them—I lost that. To be told she is pretty; she is cool; she is loved—I lost that. To have my kids running to my arms open wide—I lost that. My kids wanting me—I lost that. Moms remember times when they have prayed with their children, or comforted their children, and told them when they were hurt it was going to be all right. Powers of darkness and my own sin and addiction denied me what God intended for me. I can never replace the years that are gone. I watched people die from the drug but I never learned from that. I lost my health.

Once in my life when the pain was great I turned to drugs. Now I turn to Jesus. I read that Jesus bore my sins on the cross. I try to understand that means he bore the terrible weight of all the ugliness in my life. The terrible failure. My rebellion. I broke every commandment in the Bible. There is nothing in me that I should be loved. Yet Jesus had compassion. He is the Good Shepherd. There is a stone relief on the side of the Kokomo Rescue Mission building. It is of Jesus, the Good Shepherd. The rescue mission message is that Jesus, the Good Shepherd, leaves the ninety-nine sheep to seek the one lost sheep. I know I was the one lost sheep.

The healing this time was more painful. It was slow, but it was more thorough.

Put on the whole armor of God.

I had to make a total break from Annie. I did difficult things. I threw away all the reminders of Annie, even the gifts, things she had gotten me. Reminders. It was the only way. I broke every semblance of the relationship.

Drug court was helping. I was ordered me to write a 20-page paper on *Predators and Prey*. I had to write it and turn it in to my probation officer, Laura Rood. I was getting a different kind of education. Writing a paper was a new experience for me. I hadn't had training on how to write papers. But I worked at it. I spent hours at it. Prey allow themselves to be ensnarled. They are dependent. I learned things about myself. I made a spiritual application.

One day Ms Kem came into my room. She sat on the bed. We talked. She gave me a big hug. I realized: they were really there, the right people. I prayed that God would put the right people in my life, and He did. Amazing people. Many people had a part: Judge Menges; Matt Elkin, my attorney; Matt's wife Hillarie; Laura Rood, my probation officer; Linda Gilbert, my counselor. And of course the Kokomo Rescue Mission: Van Taylor and Dave Boss, and Ms. Kim, Ms. Krista, and Ms. Brenda.

Several days after that I went on a Sunday morning with Ms Kem and some of the ladies of Open Arms to Beulah Land Church. We did our cardboard testimony. Part of what we do is to write our addiction or our sin on one side on a cardboard, and how God delivered us on the other. I wrote for all to see: on the first side: *Sinned—homosexuality*. On the other side: *Saved by grace*. God is so good.

In March, 2010, I went to the Great Banquet for a weekend. It was a spiritual retreat. It was at the First Presbyterian Church. A number of different people associated with the Kokomo Rescue Mission are a part of this program. During the course of the weekend I had opportunity to take my guilt and shame and nail it on Jesus' cross. I did it—literally. I wrote it on a paper and with a hammer I nailed it on the wooden cross.

I had to die once again. I had to be weak so I could be strong.

> *I have been crucified with Christ, and so I no longer live, but Christ lives in me.* —Gal. 2:20

One night shortly after that I had a dream. In my dream I saw Jesus. It was the risen Jesus. I knew that because there were nail prints on his hand and a wound in his side. Jesus came to me and took my finger. He wanted me to put it on his hands, where the wounds were.

They say images of the past make their way into our dreams. There was another time, not a dream, a real time, when I was putting my finger in wounds. These were not wounds with scars;

these were open wounds. When I was in bondage to drugs my face itched from the meth. I would scratch my face. I would sit in front of the mirror and pick at those sores for hours. They were so big and ugly. They would bleed. I would put my finger on the holes in my face. I wanted to stop the blood. I wanted the wounds to go away. But they weren't going away. The sores—my sin, the powers of darkness—were destroying the face God gave me. And not just destroying my face; they were destroying me, my life, my soul. They were wounds of death. The scars on my face even today are a reminder.

But in my dream my fingers were being directed to different wounds. In the dream Jesus invited me to put my finger on the wounds on his hands. I touched them. I touched the wounds. They were scabs; I can still feel them. They were wounds healing. Those wounds were caused by nails pounded into his hands. But I know they were more. Those wounds were caused by my sins.

"By his wounds you have been healed"

—I Peter 2:24

The next day after the dream I went to church at First General Baptist. The preacher Brad Swain was preaching. The text was from John. It was the passage where Jesus came to Thomas, doubting Thomas. It was amazing. It was awesome. It was the very passage of my dream. Thomas said, *"I will not believe unless I see the print of the nails in his hands and place my hand in his side."* And Jesus appeared to him and invited him to place his hand on his side. And Thomas said, *"My Lord and my God."*

I worshipped and said, *"My Lord and my God."*

God forgave me of my sins when I accepted him as my savior back in jail. But I wasn't totally healed. That would take months, maybe years. It is still going on. The scars and the wounds of Jesus. They bring healing.

Someone explained it like pictures on the wall of my mind. The ugly past, all my sins, are recorded in those pictures. They are a reminder every day of my failings. It is so easy to push those pictures away, to hide from them, to bury them deep. But Jesus comes into the rooms of my mind. And one by one he takes down the pictures. The Bible says when we are forgiven God remembers our sins no more. (Jer. 31:33).

Is it possible that our trials and our failings can make us even stronger? I have so much joy in my heart these days. Maybe the joy is heightened because I lived so many years without joy. I have so much love in my heart. Maybe the love is heightened because I lived so many years without knowing love. I have so much thankfulness in my heart. Maybe the thankfulness is heightened because I lived so many years without thankfulness. I sense so much grace in my heart. Maybe I sense the grace because I lived so many years without knowing grace.

I do believe Jesus is in my face. He lives in my heart so why should he not be seen on my face? Everything I do I want to do for Jesus. I want to tell everyone about Jesus who can live in our hearts.

I am Cynthia Burch, and this has been my story. But it is only the first chapter of my story. I can't wait to see what God has in store in the second chapter, and the third, and the fourth.

CHAPTER 16

Things God Has Shown Me

My Bible

Take the helmet of salvation and the sword of the Spirit, which is the word of God. —Eph. 6:17

Sometimes God speaks to me through music. Sometimes I just sing, even when I am by myself, because I want to praise God. Sometimes God speaks to me through teaching, like the classes at Open Arms. Sometimes God speaks to me through nature. Even before I met Jesus I would look at the stars and know that there was something bigger out there. I saw a rainbow once and believed the promises of God. Sometimes God speaks to me in prayer.

But most of the time God speaks to me through the Bible. It was the unvarnished words of the Bible—Ephesians 6—read by my cellmate Rachel, words I had never heard before, that opened the door for my salvation.

I was blessed to have been saved in jail. I wasn't distracted by a job I had to go to, or by people I had to deal with, or by a lot of responsibilities. My jail cell was like a retreat house. All I had was God and my Bible.

The Bible I had in jail was the Bible given me by Missy Lee. It was *The New International Reader's Version Free on the Inside*. It is a Bible meant for people in jail. It included some stories of persons who found God in jail. I didn't know at that time there were a lot of translations and that there were expensive Bibles and cheap Bibles and Bibles with commentary and Bibles that were underlined in red. But I didn't need all that. I just needed one inexpensive Bible.

That Bible was the pipeline from God to me. The words of that Bible pointed me to Jesus the savior. The words of that Bible gave me encouragement in my down days. When I first heard the words of the Bible from my jail cellmates Rachel, and then Heather, I wanted more and more. I wanted to hear the stories. I wanted to hear the promises. I wanted to know all about Jesus that I could. And I wanted to read everything Paul had written, over and over.

How is it that I, who was never known as a reader, and who didn't even go to high school, and never got good grades in school, would want to read so much?

I don't know except to say that God put the desire in my heart. We have an awesome God!

My Bible is tattered and torn now. The covers are off; the pages are marked; the Bible is loose and coming apart. I don't know how much longer it will last. But even if I get a new Bible I'll never throw my first Bible away. It has been my lifeline, a gift from a great God, a love letter to his daughter Cynthia.

When Did God Start Loving Me?

I was reading in my Bible one day and I came to Jeremiah 1.

Before I formed you in the womb I knew you,
Before you were born I set you apart;
I appointed you as a prophet to the nations.
. . . .
Do not be afraid of them for I am with you and will rescue you.
—Jeremiah 1:4, 8

I know the words were spoken by God to Jeremiah. But when

I read them God lets me know they were also spoken for me. The more I learn about God the more I realize the message is not just for people long ago. The message is not just for preachers. The message is for me and for other people like me.

I really believe God knew me when I was in my mother's womb. And He never left me. Even when I was angry and rebelling and stripping and using and had no sense of right and wrong, He was at my side. I died three times. I should have died other times. I fell out on different occasions. At times I took so many drugs there is no way I should have lived. Yet, for some reason, God had His hand on me.

I suppose I could have been born in a good Christian family that loved me and took me to church and told me about Jesus. But I wasn't. Does that mean God didn't care as much for me? I don't think so. The disciples once came across a man blind from birth. They asked Jesus,

> *Rabbi, who sinned, this man or his parents, that he was born blind?*
>
> —John 9:1

Jesus answered, *Neither this man nor his parents sinned, but this happened so that the work of God might be displayed in his life.*

I wonder if God allowed me to have such a rough life so that *the work of God might be displayed in her life*. What an awesome God we have.

Friends, Who Needs Them?

Friends, who needs them?
I don't need you.
Well, maybe I do

I wrote that when I was in the seventh grade. I was alone in the world, or at least I thought I was alone. I couldn't stay at home. The kids at school made fun of me. I didn't feel close to my sisters. I had lived for nearly a year on the streets, under a bridge. I felt I couldn't trust anyone. I felt that if I were to make it I would have to do it myself.

Friends, who needs them?

I said that, but deep down I knew I longed for friends.

I had always told myself I was strong. I told myself I could deal with situations, even bad situations. I could stand up against bad influences. I was wrong. I was weak. I was susceptible to all the bad influences around me. I was exhibit #1 as a loser in the battle against the powers of the dark world and the spiritual forces of evil in the heavenly places. It was like I didn't even know there was a battle. It is like the powers would tell me to go there and I would go. Do this and I would do it. Say this and I would say it. I was like the maniac of Gadara: I was not in my right mind. I was a slave to an evil world.

When God finally reached down and touched me I realized that trying to do it on my own was not the best way. I was reading my Bible. I was reading about the disciples, how they stuck together. I was reading about the church. They loved each other.

I had assumed I would be in jail a long time. The Lord and the courts knew I had plenty of reasons for being there: drug dealing, violation of probation, identity theft. The old Cindy Burch was a menace to society. The courts didn't even know stuff I had done like robbery. Whatever my sentence I deserved it.

Then, in jail, I found out I was being considered for release. For most prisoners that would be good news. For me it brought a sense of panic. If I were released from jail where would I go? The only people I knew in Kokomo were people in the drug scene. Robbie was waiting in the wings. He would want me back and he was still in drugs. I had no family to rely on, no real friends. Every other time I had left jail I was back on drugs within the day.

I needed friends. I needed different kinds of people in my life. I needed healthy people, whole people. I needed people who would love me and accept me for who I was, and not for what they could get from me. All my life I had been around people who put me down. I needed people who could lift me up. I still had a terrible image of myself. I was still walking around with my head down.

And so I began to pray a prayer. "Lord Jesus, put the right people in my life. Put the kind of people in my life I read about in the Bible. Give me people I can talk to and I can trust. Let them show me how to live."

Then the answer came: "I have already been putting people in your life. Look around you."

I thought of Ed Swain and the people from Parr Memorial United Methodist Church who brought Christmas happiness to some little girls and showed me there were good people in the world.

I thought of the policeman who arrested me after I cried out to God for help. If that policeman had not been driving down that street on that evening, not even looking for me but for someone else—if that policeman had not arrested me I believe I would have been dead maybe even before the end of the night.

I thought of the people at Narcotics Anonymous in Las Vegas. How was it that they showed up at a vacant storefront right where I was hanging out, at that particular day?

I thought of Rachel, my cellmate, who read Ephesians 6 seven mornings in a row. How awesome is that? And Heather who read Bible stories to me. These women were in jail! They were the right people. I never would have listened to a preacher, but I would listen to someone in jail with me.

I thought of Missy Lee. Missy Lee not only knew the Bible she knew how to help a person find Christ. She is the one who told me the way of salvation. At the right time, when I was ready, God sent the right person. Missy Lee gave me a Bible.

One of the first persons I wanted to read about in the Bible was Paul—who was once Saul. Saul had persecuted Christians. Then one day Saul saw Jesus on the Damascus Road. He had a wonderful experience but he didn't understand what it meant. He still did not know how to live or what to believe. So God sent the right person into Saul's life. It was Ananias. Ananias surely did not know how important he was in God's great scheme of things. He was actually afraid of Saul because Saul was a persecutor of believers. God told Ananias to see Saul. He didn't want to do it but he was obedient. He did it. He explained to Saul the Jesus way. Rachel and Heather and Missy Lee were like Ananias to me.

God knew the prayer I needed to make was that the right people would come into my life. He was answering that prayer even before I prayed it, and then he answered it after I began to pray it regularly. The people at Richmond helped me and encouraged me. It wasn't a Christian hospital but I met Christians there. People at Richmond got new teeth for me and encouraged me to hold my head up high.

Most offenders don't look upon judges as the "right people" in their lives, but Judge Menges always seemed to know what was best for me. Sometimes what was best for me was jail. I was before him so many times. He put me in jail so many times he must have been tempted to tell them to throw away the key. But he never gave up on me. He wanted me at Open Arms. He wanted me in the Drug Court Program. He wanted me to succeed.

For sure the people of the Kokomo Rescue Mission and Open Arms were the right people God put on my path. I almost didn't make it there. I had walked away or been banned from Open Arms five different times. But when it really mattered Open Arms took me in and became my family and stood by me even in some dark times. They hugged me. They prayed for me. They loved me.

There are a host of other right people: my counselor Linda Gilbert, my probation officer, Linda Rood, and my attorney Matt Elkin. I always call him my attorney. He is really the public defender. He is not just an attorney; he is also a counselor. And with Matt I also got Hillarie, Matt's wife. She has a burden for the people Matt defends. Hillarie invited me to Bible studies. She invited me to the church she serves. I spent hours talking with her. And I need to mention Riley Case, who has helped me tell this story.

Friends, who needs them?

I do.

Isaiah 45:11

I was thinking about my kids one day. Of course I think of them a lot. I wonder what they are doing, what they are thinking, and who their friends are. I wonder how they are doing in school. I wonder if they think of me. It is always sad, because I want to be with them. Maybe I think about them too much. When I do I am aware of how I have failed them. Now I would like to make it up to them. But that is not possible. I pray for them. What hurts is that I cannot be with them to hug them and tell them I love them. I wish I could talk to them about Jesus and what has happened to me. It bothers me that other people are now moms and dads to my kids.

On that sad day I received a message, or at least an impression in my mind. Isaiah 45:11. ..Isaiah 45:11...Isaiah 45:11. The reference kept floating through my mind. I had no idea what Isaiah 45:11 says. Why Isaiah? What would Isaiah have to do with what is bothering me? And why 45:11? Why not 33:8 or 3:21 or any other passage?

I looked it up.

This is what the Lord says—
the Holy One of Israel, and its Maker:
Concerning things to come,
do you question me about my children,
or give me orders about the work of my hands?

Oh, how little faith I have! Isaiah may have spoken these words at another time and another place for another purpose, but God meant the words also for me.

...my children...

Of course. They are not Cynthia Burch's children. They are God's children. God is asking whether I am questioning Him about His children. God is telling me He knows what is best for Trent, and Angel and Faith. I know I was not a good mother. I loved my children but I didn't know how to care for them the way God wanted them cared for. So He came alongside and takes over.

I experienced new peace that day. There is still pain of course. And the ache. But my trust is in the Lord and my children are in His hands.

Fasting

I had a spiritual growth spurt in jail. Of course when you start from zero it is pretty easy to say you doubled or tripled your knowledge of God and the Bible in a week, or two weeks, or a month. I credit a lot of it to Missy Lee who led the Bible studies and the prayer group. I didn't say much at first in the group. I walked around with my eyes looking at the floor. But I gained confidence. I read the Bible. I read the Bible a lot. I found out about the concordance and so I looked up words. I think I looked up every reference to the word *prayer* in the Bible. I also thank God for uninterrupted time to pray and read the Bible. There were almost no distractions or demands on my time.

I also fasted. I knew nothing about fasting when I became a Christian. And I didn't even know what the word meant before that. But I read about it in the Bible. Some of the women spoke of it. Some of the women said they were fasting and told everyone about it. I read where Jesus said that we are not to let others know we are fasting. So I tried not to. I would give up bread, sometimes sweets, sometimes a meal. It was so I could grow closer to God.

Of course when I was on the streets I missed a lot of meals. I guess it could be called a fast, though it wasn't for God. It was because I didn't have any food to eat. In jail I had food but I would miss a meal as a way of letting God know I wanted a different kind of food, spiritual food. Jesus fasted for 40 days and 40 nights in the wilderness and was hungry. When the tempter tried to trick him into making bread out of stones, Jesus said: *Man does not live by bread alone but by every word that comes from the mouth of God* (Mt. 4:4). I couldn't fast 40 days but I could fast for several days. I did fast for six and a half months without meat.

I still fast. I fast when I have a decision to make, or when I feel I need to grow closer to Christ.

Poems From the City Jail

The Storm

Sitting in a thunderstorm, feeling all my pain,
not one person around me,
I felt alone in the rain.
Lightning strikes not once but, it seems, through my whole life,
but only because I didn't understand how to search right,
looking for all things I thought I need,
in places some may have never seen,
looking for love when it's always been right inside of me.

Give to the Lord; He will see you through;
It may not be today, tomorrow, or even in a week or two,
it's not up to you.
He does what He wants when He wants to,
He gives me so much and fills me up.

Oh Jesus, I never again want to part from you,
You are my friend; you hold my hand
and when lighting strikes you're by my side,

When I do wrong and when I do right
I feel you holding me tight.

—Cynthia Burch, July 2008
(while in jail)

Women In Jail

I saw so many girls in jail. They were so sad and angry. Some were released and then were back again. Many would be going on to prison. They were living in darkness. The beauty was there potentially, but they couldn't see it. Many had given up hope. I wanted so much to help them. If they could just find God. They could not understand why I had joy. My prayer is that they might find that same joy and be a soldier in God's army.

They come and they go,
Some you may never know;
They fade like rain in a puddle on a sunny day
Or melt like snow.
Troubled hearts you may never know,.
Not seeing Your beautiful glory.

They are weak at their lowest peak,
all of them unique.

So today I pray
for the lost, the helpless, those without faith.
I pray that some day, some way
they find You

Just a friendly face can change a day—or a nice hello—
So why do we walk away?

If you have faith pass it in a friendly wave
Or send a smile their way.
It can pull the dead from their grave,
A word of kindness can make the blindest see the way.

We have work to do
no matter who is who.
I try to do the work God sent me to.

I am a soldier in God's army.
I'm looking for recruits.

God wants all of you.
I was never strong—so scared.
I felt alone until someone passed a wave of faith.

Here I stand strong, a soldier today.
I'm full of faith,
I'm walking straight,
it's the right way.
I love everyone and would like for you to join.
Come along to a better place,

Just have a little faith.

—Cynthia Burch, November 2008

We Can Pave a Way

When I was in jail just after I had been converted I wrote a poem about hurting people. I wasn't thinking of Open Arms at the time but when I was at Open Arms I remembered the poem:

Out there a little girl cries herself to sleep each night,
a little boy has nothing to eat,
a teenage child runs the street.
A call to service is all that He needs—
Then I say, "God, call me"—
Maybe I can tell that little girl that there is more than this big world,
or share my food with that little boy who needs me to,
or help that teenager find a safe place to stay.

I don't know what God has called you to do.
I will say by God's grace,
"We can pave a way."

—Cynthia Burch, September 2008

Out of Place

Sometimes I feel so out of place
like the one wrong piece to the puzzle,
or the crooked picture on the wall
like I just don't belong,
as if I may never fit in.
It's like playing Double Dutch and waiting for the perfect moment to jump on.
You know the one moment that fits,
and I'm still standing
watching as life goes by
Trying to find it

—Cynthia Burch, November 2008
(when I first went to Richmond
and felt inadequate)

Cut Diamonds

Sometimes we don't see ourselves
Through God's eyes—
Cut perfectly in every way.

Yeah, we see the mistakes we make,
Chances we take,

But that's not what He sees.

You see,
When He sees me He says,
"She's been cut beautifully."

Everything we go through
is so the bad can be cut from us.

When he looks down
on you and me,
He sees shining beauty.

God sits back and sighs,
for we are diamonds
In his eyes.

—Cynthia Burch, September 2008
(while in jail)

LaVergne, TN USA
24 January 2011
213680LV00001B/2/P

9 781609 200145